New Hampshire
The Way I See It...

To Ellen -

Just look at the state we're in!

John Clayton

New Hampshire
The Way I See It...

John Clayton

PETER E. RANDALL PUBLISHER
Portsmouth, New Hampshire
1999

ISBN 0-9650684-3-9

These articles first appeared in the Union Leader *and are used in revised form with permission of the Union Leader Corporation*

Design by Debra Kam

Bob LaPree's cover photograph of the author was taken at Portsmouth Harbor Lighthouse at Fort Constitution, New Castle.

Produced by Peter E. Randall Publisher
P.O. Box 4726
Portsmouth, NH 03802

Additional copies available from
John Clayton
241 North Street
Manchester, NH 03104

To Nancy V.

A teacher;
She touches the future
. . . and fills my past

Contents

Acknowledgments

YOU WOULD NOT BE HOLDING this book in your hands if not for the assistance of many, many people.

There is Joe McQuaid, president and publisher of *The Union Leader*. It is he who first gave me a column, and then gave me permission to reprint them here. I am grateful.

There is Bob LaPree, photographer extraordinaire, whose work appears both on the cover of this book and on several pages within. Together, we hope our work exists as something of an evolving social history of New Hampshire.

There is Phil Vaughn, my producer at "New Hampshire Crossroads," whose energy, enthusiasm and unwavering support have allowed many of these stories to exist not just in print, but on television as well.

There are my many colleagues at *The Union Leader* and at New Hampshire Public Television who offer endless encouragement. There is my incredible family—both nuclear and extended—from whom much inspiration is drawn. There are the readers, who provide praise and damnation when either is merited and lastly, there are my subjects. Through blind faith or sheer folly, they share their stories with me so I might share them with you. They honor me with their trust.

North Country historian John Harrigan is the man you want on hand when you're planning a picaresque paddle down the Connecticut River. (Photo Courtesy of John Harrigan)

Canoeing the Connecticut

It's funny. If you hop in your car and drive south from Manchester, you can feel the tension increase with every passing mile. It starts in your neck, then moves into your shoulders, then your chest. By the time you get to New Haven, you could crack walnuts with your teeth.

When you drive north on I-93, it's just the opposite. It's soothing. Almost therapeutic. As you approach Woodstock, it's all you can do to keep your eyes on the road as you weave through the verdant valley that funnels the Pemigewasset River southward.

It's like heaven.

Only more colorful, I suspect.

And I'm only halfway there.

I'm heading all the way up to Colebrook to meet my pal John Harrigan. True, he's the only Pulitzer Prize finalist I know, but more importantly, we're working on a "New Hampshire Crossroads" piece about canoeing on the Connecticut River, and if you need a guide on the Connecticut, John's your man.

□ □ □

We're going to start our trip on Third Connecticut Lake, but first—before we begin our picaresque, picturesque paddle-fest—we have to have breakfast at the Wilderness Restaurant in Colebrook, then we have to make the drive up to Pittsburg. It's about 40 minutes as the crow flies, but no sober crow would fly over the serpentine path that is Route 145.

At first glance, the cautionary yellow highway sign that charts the course of the roadway ahead looks like a prank. It's like a corkscrew with an arrow on top.

It's perfectly accurate, mind you. It's just not the kind of sign you're accustomed to seeing when you spend most of your time south of the notches, where the roads are flat and straight and—let's say it outright—boring. That's why Route 145, which follows the lay of the land, is enough to make John wax rhapsodic.

"This road is a landscape lover's dream and a safety engineer's nightmare," he said, "but it's a road to be cherished and enjoyed."

There's one hitch, though. A small bridge is soon to be replaced, and John's afraid the whole road will wind up flat and straight and, well . . . boring.

"The point is, how far do we go to make every road as absolutely safe as possible?" he asked. "And at what point do we say that beauty and character and history come first, and it's up to drivers to adjust their driving to fit the road?"

Did I mention that John writes editorials for the *Coos County Democrat* and the *News and Sentinel* in Colebrook? I just wish the guy had stronger opinions.

□ □ □

It's quiet on Third Connecticut Lake. There's just one other boat besides John's canoe, and as we glide across the surface for the TV cameras—I imagine Curt Gowdy did a lot of this when they made the old "American Sportsman" show on ABC—it gives him a good chance to talk about the lake itself.

"Before the white man came here, this place was called Lake Sophie," he said. "She was an Indian princess, if that's the right term. One of the wives of the head man of that particular band.

"Legend is they were making their annual migration from the lower part of Coos County up to the St. Lawrence River drainage. She got sick and they spent two or three days nursing her, but she died. When they buried her, they built a large oval cairn of stones and stuck a big cedar post in it as a landmark."

No one knows exactly how long the grave stood on the wooded hills that rise from the lake, but in the 1960's, during a logging operation, a skidder operator—unfamiliar with the legend—shoved the stones aside.

Volunteers from Pittsburg eventually located the gravesite a little while ago, and a delegation from the Abenaki tribe came to sanctify the burial site.

Naturally, they stayed at John's house.

□ □ □

Unless you're a minnow, you can't get to the Connecticut River from Third Connecticut Lake, so we have to lash the canoe to the roof of John's pick-up and drive down to West Stewartstown, but first, we have to stop at Indian Stream Valley.

John wants to chat with a friend of his who runs a third generation family farm. We want to get the conversation on tape.

Unfortunately, John's friend is named John Amey. The only reason this is unfortunate is that every time the producer, Chip Neal, says "John," all three of us turn in response.

It was funny the first 11 times.

□ □ □

Fortunately, the Connecticut River is a little less serpentine than Route 145. The ride is also a lot slower and once we're out of camera range, it's just the river and John and me.

It's abundantly clear that I am the least important element.

"Normally, I just put a 75-pound rock in the front of the canoe," John said. "The nice thing about the rock is that it doesn't talk."

I turned back to make sure he was smiling when he said that. He was, but I was happy to let him do the talking. We're on his turf—or water, as it were—and the flow of information is as steady as the flow of the river.

"A lot of people have a misguided impression about this river," he said. "It's really clean and clear up here. In a way, it's one of our best kept secrets. Small-town America has led the way in cleaning up the rivers, and the headwaters have come a long way in the last four decades. Four- and five-pound fish coming out of here are not uncommon."

We're able to spot the occasional riser as we wind our way south, but we can't spend too much time admiring the scenery. While man has done what he can to keep the Connecticut clean, Mother Nature has left her marks everywhere.

Fallen trees stretch out into the river from both banks—tangible evidence of the torrential spring rains and run-off—forcing John into navigation mode. As we run through the shallows, rocks scrape against the bottom of the canoe—"hissers," he calls them—and then we're back in deeper waters.

"There's a great story about the river," John said. "I don't know if it's true, but it's too good a story to let geological facts get in the way.

"The story is there's a fault along the river valley on the Vermont side, and the theory is that it tips slightly to the west which means the water keeps chipping away at the Vermont side and depositing the soil in New Hampshire.

"To me, that means as long as the river is running, we're stealing land from those Volvo-driving socialists on the wrong side of the river," he laughed, although it occurred to me that our planned exit point—near a spot called Lunch Rock—will be on the Vermont side. Will we be safe?

"We'll be okay," John said. "There are a lot of folks in Vermont who live on the Connecticut drainage who identify more with what happens in New Hampshire than in Montpelier."

I guess that means they're on our side, even though they're on the other side of the river that binds the two states just as much as it separates them.

(Originally published Oct. 1, 1998)

To Mir, With Love

HOW TALENTED AN ARTIST is Elizabeth Carroll Smith? You might say her paintings are out of this world.

Really. One of them is in orbit even now.

It's circling about 248 miles above the Earth's surface on board the Russian Mir space station providing spiritual solace and comfort to the cosmonauts. A couple of decades ago, this might have been perceived as a treasonous act, but today, in an era of increasing harmony, Elizabeth's painting serves as a highly symbolic—and long overdue—link between technology and humanity.

"Leonardo da Vinci wrote about this a long time ago," said the artist, whose friends know her better as Betsy. "He talked about the marriage of art and science and, in essence, that's what this is."

Too bad Leonardo never met Betsy. She's a marriage of art and science all by herself. When she isn't busy working on watercolors at an easel in her Portsmouth home, she's behind the controls of a Boeing 757 as a pilot for United Parcel Service.

And what is it that launched Betsy's art career? She was the winner of a global art contest called *Ars ad Astra*. (If you flunked Latin, that means "Art to the Stars.") It's a program sanctioned by the European Space Agency—yes, they have one—that was designed to meld Europe's traditional devotion to the arts with its new forays into space.

That an American artist was selected . . . well, irony can be delicious.

In the beginning, while the odds against Betsy were not astronomical, they were considerable. All told, 171 entries were accepted, each of which was "space qualified"—shorthand for lightweight and non-toxic.

Other physical constraints? Well, for starters, there's not much space in space so sprawling murals were out of the question. Thus,

Portsmouth artist Betsy Smith's painting, entitled "When Dreams Are Born," is now on display at a Russian space station near you. (Union Leader Photos by John Clayton)

Betsy's entry was not much larger than your standard sheet of letterhead.

After a panel of earthbound judges in Switzerland winnowed the field to 20, those artists were invited overseas to witness the final judging.

"They brought us together at the Euro Space Center in Belgium where they had a video link-up with the space station," Betsy said. "A German astronaut was there with the two cosmonauts, and the 20 paintings were arranged behind them on the wall of the space station. First they narrowed it to seven, then to three, and then they said the one that would remain in orbit forever was mine. I didn't hear much of anything after that."

Her temporary hearing loss was in no way related to the roar of the Progress rocket that had carried the paintings into space, a roar that was far removed from the placid piece that has won her such acclaim.

The painting, entitled "When Dreams Are Born," is stunning in its simplicity. Two children coax a small sailboat onto a glistening pond, a pond that reflects not just a glorious full moon, but the stars and the heavens above.

The symbolism was not lost on the celestial panel of judges.

"For me, it was really an affirmation of the direction I was going in," Betsy said. "A lot of space art is very realistic and very technical, but mine is more impressionistic. I was more concerned with capturing the experience, that 'something mystical,' that spiritual element that's so much a part of space flight.

"My husband and I had been talking about what we need to survive," she added. "Yes, there's oxygen and food and water, but we also have a need for something higher, something that moves us. People aren't just technological or biological units that function without other kinds of fulfillment, and for the astronauts—who are up there surrounded by technology—maybe the image of the children provided a human element they miss."

A lot of people will be missing out if they don't pursue Betsy's work. Down in Washington, the Air and Space Museum at the Smithsonian will have an astral void without it and when prints become available, it's a natural right here in New Hampshire for the Christa McAuliffe Planetarium.

Meanwhile, we'll just let Picasso have the Prado and leave the Louvre to Leonardo. Betsy's museum is the cosmos itself. That, and the limitless space that exists in the heart of man.

(2/9/96)

President Clinton and his little friend, Ronnie Machos, had cameras snapping and on-lookers clapping when they were reunited in Manchester. (Union Leader Photo by Dick Morin)

"My Friend Bill"

WHEN SHE WELCOMED her readiness class to Highland-Goffe's Falls School last September, it took Brenda Gikas about a day to figure out that this was going to be an unusual year.

"That first day, we had show-and-tell," said Brenda. "When it was his turn, Ronnie Machos got up and told us how he was going to go to his friend Bill's house for lunch.

"I asked him if his friend Bill lived next door and he said, 'No. He lives in a big white house.' The next day, he came to class with a photograph and said 'This is my friend Bill.' And there it is, a picture of the President of the United States holding Ronnie in his arms."

To you and me, he's the President.

To Ronnie, he's just Bill—Bill Clinton—and if yesterday's reunion between these old pals didn't warm your heart, you don't have one.

It came in St. Cecilia's Hall in Manchester. The President, on a thinly-veiled campaign swing through the state, was going to address a throng of supporters. Naturally, Ronnie was in the front row.

The President gets his way on these things.

Well, most of the time.

If the President had his way on all things, America would have a national health plan and six-year-old Ronnie Machos is one reason why.

Before Ronnie was two weeks old, doctors discovered a sequence of defects in his heart. To his parents—Ron and Rhonda Machos—the term "catastrophic illness" was no longer an abstract phrase.

And, as if a child's life-threatening illness isn't worry enough, their burden was worsened when bureaucratic bungling that bordered on the criminal left them without health insurance. Within six months, their medical bills were approaching $100,000 and the Machos family was approaching bankruptcy.

Over breakfast at Belmont Hall, Ronnie's father explained his dilemma to the governor of Arkansas, a man who hoped to be President one day. To him, their plight was all too typical, and while Ron and Rhonda had hoped to enlist his aid, Bill Clinton asked for theirs instead.

Months later, Ron and Rhonda told Ronnie's story to the entire nation via satellite during the Democratic National Convention, but this isn't about mass communication. It's about letters and notes and cards, like the ones that fill Ronnie's scrap book.

The return address? The White House.

"People figured we'd never hear from him again," Ronnie's father said. "Everybody said 'You're done. The primary's over,' but here we are four years later and the President asked if Ronnie could be with him today.

"Both he and Hillary have proved again and again with their calls and their letters how much he means to them and it shows him that there actually is a president who cares about 'regular people."

So yesterday afternoon, the President of the United States swept this tiny "regular person" into his arms in a touching embrace. Cameras whirred into action and a collective sigh went up from the crowd but for that long, loving moment, they were alone together. Given Ronnie's medical history, it would be coy—but not inappropriate—to call it heartwarming.

Later on, in private, they got to chat. Ronnie asked about Chelsea and Socks and he showed Bill the pin Hillary had given him. The President showed him how it matched his cufflinks. Then Ronnie cut to the chase.

He reminded the President that Hillary, on her last visit to New Hampshire, had invited him to lunch at the White House.

The President roared.

"Well, you're welcome," he laughed, "as long as I'm there."

I wish I could be at show-and-tell tomorrow.

(2/4/96)

Hurly Burly

When you're heading up Schoodac Road in Webster, you have to keep an eye out for Little Hill Road. It's just past Lake Winnepocket, and it's the only way to get to Bob Pearson's farm.

The farm's been his home for his entire life. His folks bought it just before he was born, way back in the '20s, and it's where he and his wife Betty have raised their own kids. It's not a picture book farm though. It's a hardscrabble kind of place.

Not pretty maybe, but it works.

Just like the man who lives there.

He's got a workshop in the barn. You have to squeeze past the tractor to get in. It is probably not the kind of place you think of when you think of an artist's studio, but that's what it is, and Bob Pearson is the artist.

His medium is wood. He takes the burls from hardwood trees—those lumpy growths that mar maples and oaks and beech trees—and turns them into glorious bits of craftsmanship.

It's a special gift, this ability to turn something ugly into something beautiful, and it's a gift that Pearson—now 73—never knew he had.

"Oh, I did some carpenter work," he said, "but I wasn't a finish carpenter. I was just a barn carpenter is all."

He's been a lot of things besides a carpenter. Marine. Logger. Cop. Hunter. Farmer. Ice cutter. Selectman. Trapper. He's been just about everything you can be in Webster, but this artist thing? That's a new one.

Don't look for him to start sporting a beret, though.

"That ain't me," he laughed.

When Pearson isn't tending to his oxen or grafting wild fruit trees or doing his beekeeping or plumbing the woods for wild mush-

There is beauty in wood, even knotted misshapen burls, which Bob Pearson turns and shapes to produce glorious bits of craftsmanship on his farm in Webster. (Union Leader Photo by Bob LaPree)

rooms—"Yeah, I've done all those fool things," he laughed—he'll head into his shop.

"That's the lathe I turn on there," he said with a nod toward an ancient but still functional piece of equipment. "Anyone who turns would laugh us out of the barn if they got a look at this thing. Some of the guys that have made a name for themselves, like Peter Bloch and Gordon Keeler, they wouldn't run this for five minutes."

The lathe is about the only thing in the shop that's store-bought. Pearson even made his woodworking tools with his own hands. It's a special man who makes his own tools these days.

He keeps them on a table that's also strewn with burls—homely, gnarled, clunky clots of wood.

"This? This is a root ball from a gray birch," he said, holding up a hairy-looking ball of tangled wood. "I should probably take this to the (craftsmen's) festival at Sunapee just to show folks what I start out with. They probably wouldn't believe it."

But you believe Pearson when he talks about trees.

"Actually, the burl hurts the tree," he said. "It's like a cancer. Cutting it away does it good. If someone wants me to paint the bare spot, oh, I'll paint it, but that doesn't help the tree any. Just makes the people feel better."

Where does he get his burls? Well, unlike money, they do grow on trees, and a couple of neighbors, folks with thousand-acre farms, they let him take what he wants. He figures he's been at it for nine years now.

"In the beginning, I didn't know what I was doing," he said, and as if to prove his point, he held up a rough bowl of red oak that looked like it might possibly earn somebody a merit badge, provided the scout master was in a giving mood. He calls that a "second."

"Someone said, 'Why don't you give 'em to me?' but I burn my seconds. I try not to have any, but when I get 'em, I burn 'em.

"Now you take this one here," he said, as he turned a vase in his craggy hand. "This one's nice, but it's not going to be an A-class piece. The burl was spalted too long."

A puzzled look brings out the teacher in Pearson.

"It's like dry rot," he said. "Say in June or July, you get a good hot muggy day and you stacked some green pine logs and left them out on the ground, you'd find a blue stain on them. It's a fungus. It's like a mushroom that doesn't fruit, but in time, it destroys the wood. It makes it pretty for a while, but eventually, it's gonna rot. That's spalt."

Pearson knows his wood, but he's relatively new to this whole crafts fair thing. He needed someone who knew the ropes, so he got Lexie Shilhan and Wendy Hall to lend him a hand. They helped him set up his booth at the fairs, and they also helped him price his wares.

And how did he meet Wendy? This is Webster, after all.

"She and her husband needed someone to trap the coyotes that were getting after their sheep, and she called me," Pearson said. "You don't get to have that many friends in your life, and at my age, they get harder to find, but she's one of 'em. She's top of the pile, that lady."

Pearson doesn't exactly have a pile of finished pieces to show off. He sells most of what he makes. He has a display case in the house though, where he keeps a few of his favorites, like the bowl made out of butternut wood that's full of worm holes and three shiny bits of bird shot. He likes that one.

"I guess somebody probably shot at a squirrel in that tree for food who knows how many years ago," he said.

You won't find that piece at the Sharon Arts Center or in any of the League of New Hampshire Craftsmen shops around the state that carry his work. Nope. That one's a keeper. So is another bit of butternut, one he was able to buy back from the family of an early customer who'd passed away.

"She'd paid me $400 for it, but her daughter didn't know that," he said. "They were gonna put it in a yard sale for five dollars. I told her I'd buy it back in good faith for $400, but she said no. I finally got her to take $200. She wouldn't take any more."

There will be more pieces for sale though. Pearson still has work to do.

"I don't have time to sit on my butt," he said. "I'm too old. I'm not morbid, but I'm not going to live forever so I have to take advantage of the time I have left."

So that's why, when he gets a nice piece of walnut or ironwood, he goes out to the shop. He'll mount the burl on the lathe and shape it just so, maybe a bowl or a vase or a goblet, if the size is right. If the piece passes his personal muster, he'll carefully sand it down and then cover it with a coating of oil. Just a light coat though. Just enough to highlight the grain. Bob Pearson likes it when the character of the wood shows.

In that way, wood's a lot like people.

Character shows.

(6/18/98)

"The Rick"

NOT MANY PEOPLE get to be the definite article in sports. George Herman Ruth was "The Babe." Stan Musial is "The Man." Roger Clemens is "The Rocket." And Mike O'Malley is "The Rick."

And who is Mike O'Malley?

You'll know soon enough. This 31-year-old actor from Nashua is hovering on the brink of stardom, and a wry-but-riotous series of television commercials for ESPN may just push him over that brink.

In those commercials, Mike is cast as "The Rick," an earnest but intense—make that *very* intense—get-a-life-type sports fan who wants more than anything to convince his cable company to carry a new sports channel called ESPNews.

To sports insiders, "The Rick" has become a cult figure.

It all started as a fairly straight-forward (albeit quirky) print campaign designed to persuade cable operators to carry ESPNews. Now, it has blossomed into a full-blown, year-long, 20-commercial broadcast enterprise.

"As soon as we started running the print ads, we started getting calls from cable operators who actually wanted to talk to 'The Rick,'" laughed ESPN's Alex Kaminsky. "When you get that kind of response, you know you're on to something, and all of a sudden, we realized this would make a great consumer campaign."

All they needed was someone to be "The Rick."

Enter Mike O'Malley.

"He was amazing," Alex said. "He just walked around that room in the studio and he started coming up with stuff on the spot. He really is knowledgeable about sports, but we'd look at each other and say, 'Where did he come up with *that*?' "

Mike is the first to admit he didn't come up with *all* of it.

Meet "The Rick," the ESPN alter ego of Nashua native Mike O'Malley, whose growing success in both television and film is opening eyes on both coasts. (Photo Courtesy of NBC)

"The Rick" was the brainchild of Steve O'Brien, a Boston native who works for a Santa Monica advertising agency called Ground Zero. Perhaps it can be traced to the kindred spirit karma of long-suffering Red Sox fans, but no matter the cause, the team of O'Malley and O'Brien clicked immediately.

Mix in Christopher Guest as the commercial director—who is also a cult figure for his role in the off-beat film "This is Spinal Tap"—and you had all the makings of a momentous marketing moment.

"I think one reason people respond to 'The Rick' is because he isn't some beer-drinking, face-painting maniac, the kind Madison Avenue would portray as a typical sports fan," Mike said. "This is a guy who's just fanatical about sports, and he expresses it by collecting bizarre sports paraphernalia in the attic of his parents' house."

And just how bizarre is that paraphernalia? How about a mouthguard from hockey star Eric Lindros? Or a divot from the sixth hole at Balustrol? Or a partially torn fingernail from former Patriots quarterback Matt Cavanaugh?

"Okay, he's a little pathetic," Mike laughed, "but when I walked onto that set, saw that room and put on that Bruins jersey, I knew exactly who that guy was. When you're in that atmosphere, it's hard not to know what makes the character tick. I mean, the place is like a 13-year-old's bedroom."

But Mike, your father said "The Rick's" room looks strangely like the third floor bedroom you left behind in Nashua.

"That's why fathers should never be allowed to do newspaper interviews," he explained.

Tony O'Malley can be forgiven. He and his wife, Marianne, are understandably proud of Mike, but it's not like they want him getting a big head or anything, especially now that he's working on a major motion picture *and* a television pilot simultaneously.

The film, which chronicles the woes of air traffic controllers, is called *Pushing Tin*. The stars—Mike modestly described his own role as "non-pivotal"—are Billy Bob Thornton and John Cusack. The director is Mike Newell, whose previous credits include *Four Weddings and a Funeral* and *Donnie Brasco*.

While the film is being made in Toronto, his FOX-TV pilot is being shot in Los Angeles, yet it still strikes close to home.

"It's about a guy from Portsmouth who runs a restaurant," said Mike, who prepared for his role—unwittingly—by laboring in Portsmouth restaurants when he was a student at the University of New Hampshire. "I play a guy who kind of echoes 'The Rick,' a guy in his thirties who's trying to shed the frat-boy life style and take on a little responsibility."

The show's working title?

"It's called 'Mike O'Malley,'" he laughed. "Hey, I figured if it worked for 'Seinfeld' and 'Roseanne,' maybe it will work for me."

Mike wrote the pilot with "Simpson's" co-creator Sam Simon. It will be taped on May 1, which presents Mike's parents with a unique opportunity. Just one day earlier, his youngest sister, Kerry, will be performing in a pilot for another FOX program called "The Sue Costello Show."

"This way we can go to LA and see both tapings," said Tony, which means Mike's other siblings, Liam and Marianne, will have to fend for themselves for a while. And it will only be a little while before Mike knows his fate with FOX.

"We'll know by the second week in May," he said, "and if they go with the show, we'll probably be up soon to shoot some exteriors in Portsmouth."

Undoubtedly, that visit will include a side trip to UNH, where the dramatic arts department honored Mike with a distinguished alumnus award just a year ago. It marked a major milestone for a guy who's remarkably candid about his original motivation.

"When I was at Bishop Guertin," said Mike, who captained the cross country team his senior year, "my brother was in a couple of plays and I thought it would be a perfect opportunity to get on stage where the girls would have no choice but to watch me for a couple of hours.

"I love to have a good time," he added, "and I figured this way, I could have a good time *and* be the center of attention at the same time."

It didn't happen overnight though, this whole center of attention thing, and it's a testament to his perseverance that it's happening now.

"Granted, I've been able to make a living in TV until now," he said, "but you can't do it without a lot of help from your friends and your family. I remember when I did a commercial for 'Vivaran' about eight years ago, and everyone back home got all excited and called to congratulate me every time it was on. They keep you going.

"Now, when I graduated from UNH, if someone had told me it would be 10 years before I got my first big break, I'd have thought they were crazy. Now it's here. Ten years later. Maybe I'm the one who's crazy."

He's not crazy.

He's "The Rick."

(4/8/98)

Moses Farmer

YOU KNOW HOW you'll be watching a cartoon and then a character will get an idea and the reason you can tell he got an idea—this happens to Wile E. Coyote all the time—is because a little light bulb appears over his head?

I'm willing to wager that the same thing happened to Boscawen native Moses Gerrish Farmer back in 1859. That's when he invented the first incandescent light bulb, back when little Tommy Edison was only 12 years old.

But you say you've never heard of Moses Farmer?

There's a good reason.

"He didn't have a good PR man," said Ted Houston, a Boscawen selectman, and history buff who probably could have made Farmer a household name had he only come along a century earlier.

And why do we mention this today?

Because today is recognized around the world as National Inventor's Day. It also happens to be Thomas Edison's birthday. Gee. What a coincidence. So maybe I'm committing scientific heresy, but if Thomas Edison was the "Wizard of Menlo Park," then Farmer was the "Edison of Boscawen," and not just because it rhymes, either.

When it came to ingenuity, Farmer was every bit Edison's equal, but when it came to marketing, well . . .

"He had a fire alarm, an electric train, the whole bit, but somehow, he kept it all under a basket and never realized the acclaim he should have," added Houston, who is something like the local keeper of the Farmer flame.

He is not alone, however. Just across the Piscataqua River in Eliot, Maine, there's an equal fervor about Farmer and his findings.

First, it's important to understand the scope of Farmer's vision. This is a man who invented a four-wheel roller skate when he was a

Too bad Moses Gerrish Farmer didn't invent a camera. Then we wouldn't have to use a pen-and-ink drawing to show the New Hampshire inventor who always had a creative leg up on Thomas Edison. (Photo Courtesy of the Boscawen Historical Society)

boy of 14. Among his other early "how-come-I-didn't-think-of-that?" ideas? There's the spiked climbing spurs used by lumberjacks and telephone workers and the paper roll-down window shade.

At the risk of boring you with jaw-dropping details, his list of patents also includes the Boston Fire Alarm system, the electric train, an electric clock, the multiplex telegraph, a water-powered dynamo and for you submariners out there, the magnetic torpedo.

All of those things place Moses Gerrish Farmer in the firmament along with the other stars of American ingenuity, yet he died—while preparing an exhibit for the 1893 Chicago World's Fair—in relative poverty.

"In a lot of ways, he's the typical inventor," said Robert Gold, an inventor and the author of "Eureka! The Entrepreneurial Inventor's Guide." "We all live our lives in some inventor's dream, but the inventor who places us in that dream doesn't always profit from it."

And it isn't that Farmer was a *bad* businessman.

He was just indifferent.

And different.

"What he was was ... well, have you ever heard of a transcendentalist? That's what he was," said Ed Vetter, the town historian in Eliot, who lives right across the street from the former estate where Farmer spent much of his adult life.

"He used to sit down and cross his legs and cross his arms and maybe cross his eyes for all I know, just so he could think and meditate and think and meditate and this is what he did," Vetter said.

"Everything he invented, he gave away. He never made a nickel. He gave the inventions to other people, they'd come down, maybe they'd feed him a little something but they'd become millionaires and tell him how smart he was."

How smart was he? Well, he had to drop out of Dartmouth in 1843 when he became ill with typhoid fever, but he managed to muddle through without a degree. For instance, on one visit to Boston in 1846, he spotted a man reading a book called "Electric Magnetic Telegraphy." He bought a copy of the book for himself and on the ride home, he mastered Morse Code. Fascinated, he quit his teaching job.

Within a year, he'd created an electromagnetic locomotive driven by battery. He set up a working two-car model which he displayed throughout New Hampshire and Maine. Forty years later, Richmond, Virginia, used his model as the prototype for the first practical trolley system in America.

Meanwhile, Farmer kept tinkering with that Morse Code thing and came up with the means to use telegraph wires to report fires. After a few years spent fiddling with the application, he designed the Boston Fire Alarm System, which, when demonstrated on April 28, 1852, became the first of its kind in the nation.

For all of his various creations, however, his most visceral invention was the electric light. Think about it. If you're swimming in the ocean and you yell "Barracuda!" people say "Huh?" You yell "Shark!" and they move.

The electric light is the "Shark!" of inventions.

Farmer first demonstrated his in July of 1859 in Salem, Mass. With the mayor and city council members in attendance, he activated a galvanic battery loaded with acids and zinc for electrical current and switched on two lamps. The result:

"No matches, no danger, no care to the household," he noted. "The light was noted to be soft, mild, agreeable to the eye and more delightful to read or see by than any light ever seen before."

The problem? The battery acids and zinc cost about four times as much as the fuel needed to light gas lamps, but Farmer was convinced that gas could be eliminated as a light source—to the dismay of the Salem Gas Company—when a reliable source of electricity was in place.

That was something he worked to devise for much of his life, a life in which he seldom worried about making a living.

"And there have been millions of inventors just like him," Gold said. "There are all kinds of inventors—entrepreneurial inventors, vanity inventors, hobby inventors—but a guy like Moses Farmer is what we call an 'altruistic inventor'. That's someone who wants to make the world a better place, but who never figured out how to make it a better place for himself.

"In the end though," Gold said, "an ideal situation for an inventor is one where you don't have to be involved in the manufacturing or the marketing of a product. It's the ultimate dream of every inventor, and he had that ideal situation."

And in the end, on his death bed—when he reportedly exclaimed "Give my love to everybody, especially those on the planet Mars!"—Moses Gerrish Farmer probably died a very happy man.

(2/11/98)

Rooster Tales

So you collect celebrity autographs and photographs and you think you've got something to crow about?

Don't tell that to the "Rooster."

Like the feathered creature from which he derives his nickname, 45-year-old Doug Campbell *really* has a collection to crow about.

But he doesn't.

He lets his pictures do the talking. And what a story they tell.

Jammed inside half a dozen photo albums that are tucked inside three of his shoulder bags which are kept in his mother's Bow home is a "Who's Who" of contemporary American society, up-close-and-personal images of "People" magazine personages, the rich and famous and the high and mighty.

□ □ □

Muhammad Ali. George S. Patton III. Joan Lunden. Bob Dole. Buzz Aldrin. Barbi Benton. Alberto Tomba. Nadia Comaneci. George Bush.

□ □ □

And just what do all of these people have in common?

They have all been photographed by—and with—the Rooster.

It's an important distinction.

Unlike the Nikon-wielding, never-yielding professional celebrity chasers who create the tawdry tableau of the tabloids, this Rooster is a decidedly different animal. When he takes a photo, it doesn't count unless he's in it.

And it's never for sale.

Think of him as a "participatory paparazzi."

"But comparing me to a paparazzi is like comparing a regular

Celebrities like (clockwise, from top left) Picabo Street, Newt Gingrich, Chuck Norris, Barbi Benton, Bobby Orr and Muhammad Ali tend to keep Doug Campbell at arm's length, but only so "The Rooster" can get a better snapshot. (Photos Courtesy of Doug Campbell)

newspaper to a tabloid," he said. "My pictures are as genuine as you can get, but they're not invasive. In fact, I get very discouraged when I see some of these guys taking pictures for money. For me, if I'm not in it, it doesn't count."

□ □ □

Lee Iacocca. Peggy Fleming. Kenny G. Newt Gingrich. Chuck Norris. Sonny Bono. Zbigniew Brzezinski. Justine Bateman. Cam Neely. Haley Barbour.

□ □ □

What does count for the Rooster? Kids. All of his energy, all of his contacts, all of his focus is on kids who need help.

"'Strength. Courage. Determination.' That's what I tell the kids. That's what they need to get by," said the Rooster, whose long list of charitable endeavors runs from the Special Olympics to the Genesis Fund to the U.S. Disabled Ski Team.

His slogan has been adopted—and abbreviated—by members of the U.S. Olympic Ski Team. "SCD" is the watchword for Olympic downhill gold medalist Tommy Moe. Same for World Cup champion Picabo Street, just two of the world class skiers who regularly donate autographed skis and helmets and racing bibs to the Rooster's cause.

Whether he's in Mount Hood, Oregon or Park City, Utah, he's working for kids. If he's in Washington, D.C. or at his winter home base in the Mount Washington Valley, he's working for kids. He traces it to his own life-threatening childhood bout with hepatitis.

"That's why I'm always fighting for the little guy," he said, "but sometimes, I have to get to *these* people to get them to help the little guy."

□ □ □

Malcolm Forbes. Doug Flutie. Christopher Reeve. Sen. Paul Tsongas. Ilie Nastase. Sen. Alan Cranston. Marvin Hagler. Jack Kemp. Arantxa Sanchez-Vicario.

□ □ □

Is it charm? Is it brass? Is it sincerity? Is it *chutzpah?*

Hey, it is what it is, but no matter what you call "it," it enables the

Rooster to put one arm around his subject, extend his other arm and—more often than not—singlehandedly capture the moment for posterity.

"I have a lot of fancy 35-mm camera gear, but I never use it. I use this," he said, holding up the kind of Fuji disposable camera you can get in any corner store. "I always ask if I can take their picture. Then when I hold the camera at arm's length and get in the picture myself, they know I'm not going to sell it."

Not that he couldn't. He was offered cash for his picture with Nicole Brown Simpson after her tragic demise. No dice. Same for a picture with Robert Downey Jr. when the actor went into rehab. No sale.

"They make such a thing about these people," he said. "Why? Why can't we talk to them and say hello?"

□ □ □

Franz Klammer. Charlie Gibson. Linda Evans. Sen. Richard Lugar. Bobby Orr. Tim Russert. Egil "Bud" Kroge. "Killer" Kowalski. Sen. Phil Gramm.

□ □ □

Just saying "hello" works for the Rooster, an inveterate letter writer who often sends copies of his photos to the stars who enter *his* gravitational pull.

In return, he frequently gets handwritten notes from the likes of former First Lady Barbara Bush, Former Patriots' quarterback Steve Grogan and former Vice President Dan Quayle, who spelled Rooster—I swear—with just one "O."

"He just has a contagious, infectious presence that makes people like him," said former U.S. Rep. Bill Zeliff, who watched with awe—and pleasure—as the Rooster infiltrated Bob Dole's inner circle during the 1996 Presidental Primary.

"I'm sitting there watching Bob Dole make his concession speech," said Tom Eastman, an editor of *The Mountain Ear* in North Conway, "and there's Rooster, right there on stage with him. I couldn't believe what I was seeing."

He should have. The Rooster knows everyone. And I mean *everyone.* He even introduced Eastman to his girlfriend.

"And I have the pictures to prove it," Rooster laughed.

□ □ □

Billy Kidd. Bob Dornan. Bernie Carbo. Elizabeth Dole. Mario Cuomo. David Hartman. Guillermo Vilas. Dennis Connor. Kyle Petty. Michael Andretti.

□ □ □

So just who is this Rooster?

Who is this gentle soul who once won the "Cast Iron Stomach" award for consuming 125 jalapeno peppers at Nothin' Fancy Restaurant at Weirs Beach? Who is this guy who once performed a wedding service atop a Canadian mountain peak for a Warren Miller ski film? Who is this man who has asked that, upon his death, his ashes be scattered upon Tuckerman Ravine?

By his own admission, he seems to be a cross between omnipresent fictional figures who became witnesses to history, movie characters like Tom Hanks' "Forest Gump" and Woody Allen's "Zelig." Is the Rooster a character himself?

"If you mean character in the sense that I can reach out to all types of people and feel comfortable with them, then I'm a character," he smiled. "And all this computer enhancement stuff with pictures? That's like robbing a bank. You have to have your picture taken with them for real."

For years, his photos sat in piles around his house until one day, he got a piece of advice from another photographer, some guy named David Hume Kennerly.

"He told me I should put them all together," Rooster said. "He thought maybe I should put them into a book."

The perfect title?

How about "Rooster Tales."

(9/25/97)

Because of his old world work ethic, there's just as much soul as sole attached to the shoes that are carefully handcrafted by Cordwainer Paul Mathews. (Union Leader Photo by Bob LaPree)

The Cordwainer

WHY WOULD PEOPLE CHOOSE to purchase handmade, custom-fitted shoes from a craftsman like Paul Mathews? Certainly it has as much to do with the soul of the man as the soles of the shoes.

For three generations, his family has fashioned the finest of shoes for a most discerning clientele, and while he occasionally looks back on his own career—it's a view that spans 66 years—he prefers to look ahead.

"How old am I?" he smiled. "I'm 78, I think. But I'm not about to retire."

You can't imagine how much relief that statement brings to people. Almost as much relief as his shoes bring to the folks who couldn't bear footwear that didn't come from the Deerfield farmhouse that is home to The Cordwainer Shop.

The Cordwainer name may not ring bells like Bass or Florsheim, but that doesn't matter to Mathews. While those giants crank out shoes by the thousands, his shop makes just six pairs per day. The result? His professional imprint is in the footprints left by his clients, be they Oscar winners like Michael Douglas, Emmy winners like Valerie Harper or Grammy winners like Carly Simon.

Like most of his clients, those celebrities have come to know his wares through a series of national expositions, exclusive trade shows—many of them invitation-only affairs—that bring out an equally exclusive shopper.

"We were at a show in Boston when Carly Simon picked up a pair of Victorian boots," said Mathews' wife, Molly Grant. "She said 'These are the most beautiful shoes I've ever seen,' so right away, I asked her, 'Can I tell people that?' She said, 'Sure.' She ordered four pairs of shoes that day."

And what is it that so enthralls customers like Lindsay Wagner, Sally Jessy Raphael and William F. Buckley? In part, it's the fashion, since the shoes can be made in 20 different styles, but first and foremost, it's the fit.

"In the beginning, my father simply wanted to make shoes that were good for feet," Mathews said. "He was a book salesman, and when he was walking door to door, his feet would hurt so bad he'd have to take his shoes off and stick his feet in the horse trough.

"He learned the hard way that shoes weren't being made for feet. They were made for fashion, and he just wanted to relieve the suffering of the world."

And Edward Mathews did just that by developing something called the "Antioch shoe," which boasted a low heel and a rounded toe. Sounds simple enough.

"But at the time, in the 1920s, it was just the opposite of the prevailing fashion," Mathews said. "That's when all of the flappers were wearing those atrocious shoes with the high heels and pointed toes."

Right on the heels of his invention, however, came the Great Depression. That, and an injunction from manufacturing giant International Shoe, prevented him from making the shoes that he had designed.

In time, he bounced back and started his own small shop in Weymouth, Mass. That's where Paul first got tied up in the business at the age of 12. By high school, he was supervising half a dozen workers and after World War II, he and his brother were running the business themselves.

It wasn't until the early 1950s—on a long, leisurely return trip from Canada—that Mathews first set foot in Deerfield. He was already taken with the old colonial town when he stopped at an antique shop in the town center and asked, almost on a whim, if there were any properties for sale.

"This one is," the shop owner replied.

So Mathews bought it. On the spot. By 1967, he and his two sons had acquired the 300-acre plot that is now the Wild Orchard Farm.

That's where Cordwainer—it's from an archaic word for shoemaker—has been housed ever since, in the expanded and renovated farmhouse Mathews built with his two sons, Rob and Jamie. Today they're also his co-workers, as is his daughter Sara. It's a family business in every sense, and the customers are made to feel like kin as well.

The late Bill Loeb was one such customer. So was Olympic figure skater Sonja Henie. Same for auto magnate Henry Ford. ("When he died," Mathews said, "the story in Life magazine made reference to the soft-soled shoes he always wore.")

More contemporary clients include actress Demi Moore, comedian Bill Murray, rock stars Steve Tyler and Joe Perry from Aerosmith and let's not forget Jerry Mathers (as in "The Beaver").

To be sure, the cost of the shoes may frighten the frugal—sometimes they run as high as $365 per pair—but Mathews' ability to renew and restore them is tantamount to a lifetime warranty. Besides, his clients appreciate the simple, distinctive trait that sets Cordwainer shoes apart from all others.

"The only real problem in shoemaking is attaching the upper to the sole," Mathews explained. "Most often, it's glued or cemented, but it can't breathe. The unique feature of ours is that it uses no cement, and people feel it immediately. It's pretty funny, really. After they try them on, they'll start beckoning other people to come try them. That's gratifying."

Also gratifying is the response to the weekend workshops the family now conducts at the farm. Guests stay right on the grounds—only two at a time, thank you—and learn to make their own shoes by hand. It's a calming complement to the mail order business and the 30 trade shows that Paul and Molly attend each year.

Of course, if your name isn't on the guest list for those exclusive shows, you can always look for the Cordwainer booth when the League of New Hampshire Craftsmen holds its annual show at Mount Sunapee in August.

It should be worth the wait. As one satisfied customer put it, there's no joy like finding new shoes that feel like old friends.

(2/20/97)

Much like the pieces on his chessboard, Josh Friedel's future in the world of chess is all in front of him. (Union Leader Photo by John Clayton)

The Prodigy

IF YOU THINK the "Sicilian Defense" is a courtroom ploy for attorneys representing the likes of John Gotti, then I've been successful in using the phrase as my opening gambit.

See, I'll do anything to lure you into a piece about chess—the "Sicilian Defense" is one of the game's more celebrated strategies—and the fact that you've read this far means it's working.

A lot of people won't read a story about chess. Some people who know the game find it intimidating. Folks who aren't familiar with it think chess is nothing more than checkers with lace curtains. And an attitude.

Hal Terrie knows better.

"People have described it as an art form," said Terrie, 46, who is president of the New Hampshire Chess Association, "but really, it's the closest thing I know to a direct struggle between two minds."

And he won't mind if you find your way to the Center of New Hampshire Holiday Inn this weekend. That's where the NHCA will host the 21st Annual Queen City Open, a tournament that will bring more than 100 of New England's top chess players to Manchester. Play begins tomorrow at 10 a.m. Spectators are welcome.

One of the more fascinating sub-plots of the tournament revolves around Josh Friedel, a 10-year-old from Goffstown who is the reigning national champion in his age group.

Last May, he prevailed over 270 opponents in the kindergarten to third-grade level to claim top honors at the National Elementary Chess Championship in Tucson. A previous winner of the same event, Josh Waitzkin, inspired the film "Searching for Bobby Fischer" (which you should see, even if you don't know a Grandmaster from a ghetto blaster).

Like Waitzkin, Friedel is a child prodigy with a prodigious appetite for the game. He started playing—at his own insistence—at the age of three. Today, his point rating of 1,928 has him on the threshold, age notwithstanding, of the state's top 20 players.

He may well cross that threshold this weekend.

"I think Josh can become a Grandmaster," said Terrie, who plans to pit his prized pupil against some formidable opponents this weekend as part of a continuing grooming process.

All of which is fine with young Josh, incidentally.

"I prefer playing against grown-ups," he explained, without so much as a hint of arrogance. "You can learn more playing against grown-ups. They're more experienced. The others just fall for tactics."

Tactics are a grand part of this game, which traces its roots back to 6th-century India. In spite of that long history, while hard-core devotees eat, sleep and breathe the game, it appears only intermittently in the consciousness of the general public, as when Bobby Fischer bested Boris Spassky in 1972 or when Garry Kasparov recently out- smarted the IBM Deep Blue computer.

Accordingly, the man on the street might be able to name two or three great chess players—go ahead, try—whereas the chess aficionado could rattle off names as if he were managing a Grandmaster Rotisserie League.

And that man-on-the-street reference? That's not gender bias showing through. For some inexplicable reason, women are noticeably absent from the chess scene at the local, national and global level. Of the 450 Grandmasters in the world, only six are women and, right here at home, of the 100 top-ranked players in New Hampshire, only one woman—Joan Schlich—makes the grade.

"Far be it from me to butt up against any politically correct attitudes," Terrie said, "but that's typical around the country and the world. For whatever reason, women and girls tend not to gain or maintain an interest in the game as do males.

"There's no reason they can't do it," he said, citing the success of the three Pogar sister from Hungary, "but even in scholastic chess programs for girls, there is a considerable drop-off after the age of 14."

A similar age-related obstacle may soon confront Josh Friedel.

"With every young player, there's a point around age 13 or 14 where, if they want to go further, they have to buckle down," Terrie said. "Not everyone who has the talent has the drive or the determination. At the highest levels of the game, there are brilliant, talented players who will never have a shot at the world championship because they don't have the desire."

Does Josh have it? Who knows? But his parents—Lynn and Seymour Friedel—know they want him to enjoy as normal a childhood as possible. That means school and soccer and football and sailing. And responsibility.

"We have a deal if he wins money at a tournament," said his mother. "I pay his entry fee, but if he wins more than the fee, he has to pay me for half of it. We started that when he started winning big money."

Of course, no one goes into chess for the money.

"One of the great things about the game is its effect on developing critical thinking skills," Terrie said. "Formal academic studies have shown that chess is better than intense reading programs or computer studies. It's better not only in terms of producing better grades, but even in disciplinary cases, introducing chess has led to extraordinary changes in those students."

Toward that end, the NHCA is intent on bringing chess to schools around the state. It offers free boards ("Of course, our funds are not unlimited," Terrie cautioned) and assistance for schools that wish to begin instructional programs.

That program may not produce another Josh Friedel, but it may produce the kind of climate that allows someone like him to thrive. Something like the atmosphere Gene Crews has created in his classroom at the Mountain View Middle School in Goffstown.

"Mr. Crews is reading a book about chess now. He says he's going to beat me," Josh said. Then he grinned.

(2/28/97)

Vic Moulton's days begin and end at his woodpile, which is the only form of advertising he needs outside his shop in Rochester. (Union Leader Photo by John Clayton)

The Woodcutter

HOW MUCH FIREWOOD does Vic Moulton have? He's got stacks of it. Tons of it. You might even say he has wood to burn. Anyone who's ever made the winding drive from East Rochester into Maine along Route 202 can tell you that.

There's no sign outside his shop, but then again, he doesn't need one. The heaping piles of logs and endless stacks of cordwood provide all the signage he needs in these parts.

"I'm just an old-fashioned firewood producer. Nothing spectacular," he says with a shrug. "It's getting the wood here, working it up and getting it to the customer. That's all."

Actually, that's not all. There's a lot more to the job than meets the eye. There's also a lot more to Vic Moulton.

In the course of his 70 years, he's done more good work with wood than Noah. Or Babe Ruth. Or Bob Vila. Unfortunately, it's hard to document. Most of his work has gone up in smoke. But it's supposed to.

Every year, he puts up about a thousand cords of wood. His schedule couldn't be simpler. His work week? It never ends. No weekends. No holidays. He works 365 days a year.

It's simple.

He doesn't work?

He doesn't eat.

"I went to see my boy down in Massachusetts on Christmas last year," he said, "but I put up two cords of wood before I went. Good thing too. There were people waiting for me when I got back. Sometimes people wait till the last minute for things. We're all culprits, I guess."

Like many folks who engage in hard physical labor, Moulton finds great dignity in his work. There's also a great dignity to the man himself, although it's carefully concealed beneath the grit and the grime.

"I guess I'm not too photogenic," he grinned.

He knows his limitations. But not as well as he knows his wood.

"See that knot configuration?" he said, pointing to a gnarly oak that stood out amongst a grapple load of logs. "That's a great burning unit. The fiber's a lot more dense than the other smooth stuff, but it looks so grotesque that some people don't want it. People want aesthetics. It may not be pretty, but it's unsurpassed for burning."

So he burns it. His tiny cottage is heated solely with wood.

"Yep, I burn the 'undesirables,'" he said. "No fossil fuels. I got a little electric heater in case of an emergency, but I don't need it. If it gets too cold, I just stoke my stove."

It's an ancient stove, but his is an ancient trade. And to hear Moulton tell it, his equipment is equally ancient.

"That truck? It drinks like a sailor on a Friday night," he said. "It's that fuel these days. It used to get seven miles to a gallon. Now I'm lucky to get three when I have a load on 'er.

"And my splitter? I just had to get it fixed. It cost me $400. I would have fixed it myself but I'm not too good on that electronics stuff. In the old days, oh, I used to just belt the hell out of the wood with an old ten-pounder," he smiled while miming his way through a maul swing, "but I'm getting too old for that."

His product line is as simple as his schedule. He deals in oak, maple and beech. He does keep a small pile of hickory on hand—"In case someone wants to smoke a pig," he explained—but he's careful to avoid soft woods.

"No pine or hemlock or spruce," he said. "You take a wood with a lot of tar resins and if you're not up on your propensity of woods, it can come back on you. Especially if you're asthmatic."

Next thing you know, he's explaining the principle of "volumetric efficiency" and the sparkle in his eye makes you realize he couldn't be happier if he was reading Robert Frost, who wrote about people just like him.

"I know it looks and sounds laborious, which it is at times," he admitted, "but a lot of people don't understand what goes into cutting and splitting wood. And I get a great deal of pleasure out of the independence. I'm the boss. I earn my way. That's all. That's all I know."

(12/12/96)

Risqué Business

SO YOU'RE RICH LEDERER, one of America's foremost linguists and your love of language knows no bounds.

You've written a dozen critically acclaimed books that embrace spoken and written English with a passion that borders on lust, but—speaking of lust—you know that some of the world's most fascinating word play has been devoted to racy, ribald, off-color stories which you've been collecting over the years in your Concord home and now you want to put them in a book.

The biggest problem? If you don't include the search for a willing publisher, it's coming up with a title, but you are, after all, Rich Lederer, so you employ all of your cunning and occasionally stunning punning power and you narrow the field to three possibilities:

- *Filthy Rich,*
- *Meanwhile, Back at the Raunch,* and;
- *Nothing Risqué, Nothing Gained.*

Okay, he also had a fourth title in mind, but there's *no way* I can tell you here, so he settled on *Nothing Risqué, Nothing Gained.* There's an irony there too, because the truth is, he risked a lot, but we'll get to that later.

"Personally, my first choice was *Filthy Rich,*" he laughed, "but it might not have meant anything to you if you're one of the billion people wandering the planet who've never heard of Rich Lederer."

It's hard to imagine that there are a billion people who haven't heard of New Hampshire's premier wordsmith—the author of *Anguished English* and *Get Thee to a Punnery*—who stopped at the Cambridge Book Stop in North Manchester recently to meet and greet his readers.

And their response to his randy writings?

"I never had a book that sold like this," he said with a grin.

Readers were racing to get copies of linguist Richard Lederer's raciest book, a compilation of bawdy humor he almost entitled "Filthy Rich." (Union Leader Photo by John Clayton)

And why not? This isn't one of those "There once was a man from Nantucket ..." anthologies. Well, at least I didn't find that one. In its place, however, are riddles and rhymes and loads of lecherous, lascivious limericks which are—if you can believe it—politically correct.

Up to a certain point, anyway.

"It's because I believe jokes should be obscene but not hurt," he cracked, which was his way of explaining the omission of homosexual jokes, AIDS jokes, racial jokes and religious jokes, among others.

That still leaves plenty of material to raise eyebrows out there, but it's not like Rich is venturing onto virgin territory. Great writers have often embraced the racy. The body and the bawdy have both been fair game for Geoffrey Chaucer, William Shakespeare, Alexander Pope and Jonathan Swift, so why, he asks, should Rich Lederer miss out on what he calls "good, clean dirty fun."

He almost did though.

"Publishers kept telling me that I was supposed to be a tweedy professor," said Rich, who earned that distinction by spending 27 years on the faculty of the prestigious St. Paul School in Concord before leaving in 1989 to write full-time.

"They said people saw me as a straight-laced teacher from a church boarding school. They were all terribly worried about my reputation, but I told them 'Hey, it's *my* reputation. Let *me* take the chance."

So he did. And now, 21 manuscript rejections later, readers can't get enough of it. At least those readers who have reached the age of consent.

And for those who object?

"I've received virtually no negative response to this book," he said, "but if people are offended, well, no one is making people buy this book or read this book, and if they think it is somehow inconsistent with my previous work, they don't know it very well. People who are familiar with my work will recognize the double-and triple-entendres and know that this is totally in line with what I do.

"When you see an occasional dirty joke, it can seem sordid, but when you see 300 pages grouped by classification, you begin to say, my Lord, this is really part of who we are as Americans. It's part of our folklore, and I'm as proud of this book as anything I've done.

"I know there are people, in Manchester who agree with me," he smiled. “When I spoke at the Rotary and Kiwanis, I couldn’t bring enough books with me and in some ways, I hope my readers will gain a new respect for me. It’s not easy to keep finding synonyms for the male anatomy, you know.”

(2/23/96)

Say Cheese!

You know what gets my goat? People who won't try goat cheese. When you broach the subject with these people, the reaction is fairly predictable. First they make a funny face, then you can see them mouth the words—*goat* cheese?—and then they shake their head in horror.

It's like they think goat cheese is a dangerously hip-and-trendy passing yuppie fad, like retro sideburns or Capri pants. As if Aristotle and Socrates and Plato didn't eat goat cheese over two thousand years ago.

Okay, maybe they didn't eat it the way we eat it today, as hazelnut-crusted goat cheese souffle or warm arugula with goat cheese and sun-dried tomatoes—can you tell I've been reading "Bon Appetit" again?—but they ate goat cheese nonetheless, and, since all three of them are among the great thinkers in the history of the world, *ipso facto,* I guess we can safely conclude that eating goat cheese will make you *very* smart.

Either that, or I'm overlooking the toga factor.

Anyway, if you have the nerve or the verve to eat or serve goat cheese, you should know about a goat cheese from these parts. In particular, I'm thinking of a brand called "Udderly Delicious" which is produced at the Nunsuch Dairy in South Sutton.

That's where Courtney Haase keeps her herd of Swiss Toggenburg milking goats. There are 19 milk producers now—the 14 kids are pretty much along for the ride—but by next year, she plans to increase the milking herd to 30.

It's a bold move for a micro-dairy like hers, but if it weren't for bold moves, Courtney wouldn't be running Nunsuch Dairy.

You're waiting for the story behind that dairy name, aren't you?

"I used to be in a convent," she smiled. "It was with a cloistered Franciscan order. Now all my goats are named after nuns I lived

Goat farmer Courtney Haase enjoys the attention of her flock every bit as much as her customers savor the flavor of the cheese she produces at her farm in South Sutton. (Union Leader Photo by Bob LaPree)

with at the monastery. Well, all except Antoinette. She's the only one who's not named after a nun, but the woman she's named after? She should have been. She was a saint."

Some would say the same of Courtney.

"She's a remarkable woman," said Steve Taylor, commissioner of the state's Department of Agriculture, who presented Nunsuch Dairy with a "Farm of Distinction Award" last year.

"There are several goat dairies up in the Connecticut River Valley," he said, "but they put their milk up for sale at a plant in Barre, Vermont. Ten years ago, Courtney decided she wanted to milk her own goats and make her own cheese. They said it couldn't be done, but she's done it."

As proof, you might consider the tony restaurants where they serve her cheese. It's in dishes at places like Henrietta's Table at the Charles Hotel in Boston and at the Kendron Valley Inn in Woodstock, Vermont.

Closer to home, they serve it at La Meridiana in Wilmot and at the Bedford Village Inn, but the best way to understand and appreciate the success of her enterprise is to visit her five-acre farm on Route 114.

Once you get past the peacocks and the ducks, head for the milking stall just off the barn. That's where Courtney coaxes her goats every day, twice a day for nine months of the year. (They get a break from December to March.) Once she gets them munching contentedly from a pail of grain, she uses an automatic milking machine to draw about three quarts of milk from each of them. It's here where she seems most at home, talking about the goats, the farm and the business she never really envisioned.

"When I first got started, I had no intention of being a licensed dairy," she said, "I thought I'd just have enough milk for myself, but once I got up to six goats, I had to decide what to do.

"I couldn't afford to keep them as pets and I never did show them, so I just started looking for equipment to process the milk and make cheese," she added. "That was the hardest part. There was no small-scale dairy equipment."

And what constitutes small scale? For Courtney, it was a mini-vat she found in England, and even that was too small. Eventually, she found a dairy designer in North Carolina who created the 25-gallon pasteurizer that is at the heart of her business.

If the pasteurizer is the heart, the goats are the soul.

"Once I start milking a goat," she said, "I try to keep her in the herd. I will sell my kids, but I won't sell my milkers. It seems I keep them all for a reason though. Most of them are good milkers but some are just good friends."

You say you can't have too many friends?

You *can* have too many goats.

"A lot of people think the more goats you have, the more milk you produce and the more money you make, but there really is a breaking point," she said. "For me, I know now that it's between 30 and 33 goats. It's one thing if you're going to sell your milk to a processing plant, but it's another thing to process it all yourself, especially when you're also the herd manager and cheese maker."

And it is there where Courtney shines.

Immediately after the milk is drawn from the goats, it goes into a bulk tank where the temperature is quickly reduced from 90 degrees to 40 degrees. Next, it's transferred to the pasteurizer. Starter and rennet are added to the mix, which is incubated overnight.

The next day, Courtney draws off the contents of the tank and—using two layers of cheese cloth—she separates the cheese curds from the liquid whey. When the cloths are filled, she has a pumpkin-sized ball of cheese. By the time the tank is empty, she has 25 of those cheese orbs draining from an overhead rack.

By morning, the cheese exists in its unadulterated form. She'll flavor and spice some for sale in her own farm shop, but the raw product is shipped to restaurants where the chefs are free to create their own magic.

"They can sweeten it with sugar and honey, fresh berries or maple syrup," she said. "I have one restaurant that uses it in tortellini with sun-dried tomatoes and roasted peppers, and another that serves it on miniature pizzas.

"I even sell little two-ounce containers, so if a restaurant wants to put it in their bread basket, they can use that instead of butter. The high-end restaurants like that because it's just a little extra touch of class."

Speaking of classes, an inordinate amount of Courtney's time has been spent in schooling future micro-dairy operators. It's what prompted her to create the Small Dairy Project, a non-profit group that has members in 37 states, including Hawaii.

"I'm trying to get funding for an instructional video now," she said, "just so other people won't have to go through everything I went through. People ask me if I'm afraid of the competition, but I'm happy to help them. Maybe it's part of my monastic training. Besides, I can't make enough cheese to keep up with demand.

"I tell people my biggest competitors are John and Olivia Walton," she smiled. "We'll watch 'The Waltons,' and my mother will say, 'How come they don't have a manure problem?' and 'How come they never have too much work to do?' That image of the idyllic farm? *That's* hard to, compete with."

Almost as hard as keeping up with the demand for her product.

"Last year I ran out of cheese in December and it cost me a restaurant," she said, "so I'm going to add more goats, but I know what my limits are. I may not make a million dollars, but I want to be sure I'm making a million dollar product."

(5/20/99)

The Singing Cop

In case you missed it, they're celebrating a centennial down at the Hampton Beach Casino Ballroom this summer but so far, all of the commemorative stories I've seen have focused on the high-powered headliners who've performed there through the years.

It's understandable.

With the possible exception of Frank Sinatra, the Casino has played host to just about every big-time show biz luminary you can name. We're talking Duke Ellington, Harry James, Count Basie, Patti Page, Willie Nelson, Wayne Newton, Tina Turner, Roy Orbison and Ray Charles, and that's just for starters. The list spans the generations, from Sammy Kaye to Robert Cray.

If you're star struck, that list may get your juices flowing, but me? I've been waiting in vain for a story about a lesser-known but no-less-colorful seaside singer, one my parents have raved about down through the years, so I guess it's up to me to tell you about Bill Elliot.

Perhaps you know him better as "The Singing Cop."

He's not a cop anymore, but at 94, he's still an arresting presence. And he doesn't sing anymore either, but a morning in Bill's company can be as entertaining as all get out. And I got out to his house in Hampton recently.

"Oh, I guess I stopped singing about 40 years ago," he said. "I had a tumor on my vocal chords, something they call a 'singer's node.' About a year after I had it removed, I could sing again, but I just didn't sound like me, so I didn't sing in public much anymore. I can still carry a tune and I still sing in church, but that's enough."

But they couldn't get enough of Bill back in the '20s, '30s, '40s and '50s.

Maybe it was his arresting stage presence, but people who heard Bill Elliot sing at Hampton Beach will never forget "The Singing Cop." (Photo Courtesy of Bill Elliot)

On a typical Sunday evening, Bill would be out in full police uniform directing traffic on Ocean Boulevard, right between the Casino Ballroom and the Bandstand when the conductor—frequently Hal McDonnell—would beckon him up to the stage. After dodging through the traffic, Bill would bound up to the microphone and wow the crowd with a tune or two before returning to his duties.

Tourists may have marveled at the notion of a cop who could sing, but locals knew they were watching a singer who just happened to be a cop. They'd known that since 1921 when Bill Elliot stepped onto that same Bandstand stage and—using a megaphone instead of a microphone—won the first Hampton Beach Amateur Night at age 16. After that, his legend grew and grew.

Not to belittle that Hampton Beach acclaim, but Bill's real breakthrough came in Boston in 1936. He was on stage singing a difficult aria—for you Rossini fans, it was *"Largo al factotum"* from "The Barber of Seville"—and just for good measure, he sang it in Italian. Unbeknownst to Bill, the audience included a talent scout named Ted Mack—yes, *that* Ted Mack—and the future host of the "Original Amateur Hour" promptly ushered Bill into the big time.

"They booked me onto 'Major Bowe's Amateur Radio Program' in New York," Bill said. "I know I was a little nervous because I always got a little nervous before I sang, but Major Bowe came up and told me, 'I have a feeling they're really going to like you.'"

Sure enough, Bill—clad by then in the uniform of the Hampton Police Department—stepped on stage at the CBS Theatre on Broadway for the live, coast-to-coast broadcast and sang a popular standard called "Love in Bloom." For all we know, the phones may still be ringing.

"It was the first time in the history of the program they ever asked anyone to come back and sing an encore," Bill smiled. "I don't know whether that many people really called or if he just made it up—he really built me up big—but he insisted I go back on, so I performed the Rossini aria again."

They should have billed him as "The Opera Cop."

The response of the home audience was exceeded only by that of the 1,500 in the studio. It probably goes without saying that Bill won that night's competition and he was asked to go on the road with one of Major Bowe's traveling shows. After a single performance at the Metropolitan Theatre in Boston, however, he decided that life on the road wasn't for him.

"Back then, I had a wife and two kids and a job," he said.

The job—well, one of them anyway—was right there in Boston. He had a radio program on WEEI where he was both a host and a "dialectitian." Not only would he sing with Ruby Newman's Orchestra—in seven languages, mind you—but he would also take part in live, on-air skits that tested his oratorical gifts.

"On one of the skits, we would pretend to visit a different country every week and I would do the accent of the other country," he said. "We always had an audience in the studio, and there was an Army colonel there for one show when I was doing an impression of Hitler.

When the skit, was done, the colonel came over and said, 'You may be all right, but you sure sound like a kraut.' I made sure he waited for the end of the show when I sang 'God Bless America.' After that, he said I must be okay."

He was better than okay. Even though he was commuting from Hampton to Boston, he still received regular overtures from national broadcasting outfits, overtures he managed to resist until 1941.

"I really thought it was my big break," he said. "I signed a contract with Procter & Gamble for a radio program. We were going to do live shows and record them on discs that would air five days a week from coast-to-coast and up into Canada."

For such a clean-cut character, it should come as no surprise that his primary underwriter was Lava Soap. It may surprise you, however, to know that early ratings for his program were matching or topping such radio institutions as "Inner Sanctum" and "Amos 'n' Andy." For a while, anyway.

"I think we had done three of the discs," Bill said. "Then the Japs attacked Pearl Harbor. I don't know what it was, but there was something in Lava Soap that the Army needed, so they took it off the market. Without any Lava Soap to sell, Procter & Gamble canceled the program. Sixty other programs got canceled at the same time, so in a way, I guess I consider my show to be a casualty of war."

It says a lot about Bill Elliot that he can smile when he tells that story, but he knows he has plenty to smile about. He's still married to his wife of 72 years, the former Alzena Leavitt of the Hampton Leavitts. They've lived in the same house—built by his father—for all of their years together, years in which they raised their family (one that grew to include three children, all told) and years in which they devoted their lives to the town that they love.

That devotion shows up in town histories, like Peter Randall's *Hampton: A Century of Town and Beach,* which notes that the end of the 1937 summer season was celebrated as "Bill Elliot Week." Peter also recounts what must be the American equivalent of a command performance, when Bill sang a solo before a special session of the New Hampshire Legislature.

In this, the Casino's centennial year, it's good to acknowledge Bill's indelible tie to the old ballroom and the Hampton Beach Bandstand, but for those who saw him sing, it's the beautiful baritone and the arresting presence of "The Singing Cop" that will serve as Bill Elliot's legacy.

(5/20/99)

A Taste of Tripe

I shall never forget my first encounter with tripe.

It was February of 1971. I was in France on a school trip. (Seventy-two girls. Seven boys. And you people wonder why I love Paris so much? But that's another story for another time.)

Anyway, the hotel management was somehow deluded into thinking we were worldly, sophisticated Americans, because the first night we had dinner, the waiters went around the table and before each of us, in the meticulous style of European table service, they placed a generous serving of tripe.

Seventy-nine hearty portions of tripe.

Of course, we didn't *know* it was tripe. Fortunately, one student—a biology major, I'm sure—recognized it for what it was.

For all I know, mine's still there on the table.

The stampede from the dining room probably looked like we were emulating the poor bovine beasts from whom the tripe had been harvested.

Unless you count my writing, my second encounter with tripe came yesterday, and I wasn't in Paris. I was in Epping at Rosie's Diner on Route 125. For years, I have been driving by Rosie's, deliberately ignoring the outdoor marquee that lists the specials served inside, primarily because one of those specials is tripe.

Specifically, it's fried tripe.

I would have happily continued this trend of willful indifference, but then my friend Steve Taylor—he runs the state Department of Agriculture—put together a list of 100 things to do in New Hampshire, and sure enough, right there at number 100, he suggests that, to know the *real* New Hampshire, we should "eat at any diner that still serves good fried tripe."

I've been ruminating about this for weeks, not unlike a cow with

The rubbery texture of tripe is no match for the determination of Tony Sanchez-Young, who tackled an order of the organ meats at Rosie's Diner in Epping. (Union Leader Photo by Bob LaPree)

his cud, which, come to think of it, is a highly appropriate simile because ... well, because tripe is what a cow *uses* for ruminating. It's the light-colored, rubbery lining of the stomach, and the very thought of eating it is still enough to turn my own.

So I called Steve and asked him why he felt it was such an important rite of passage for a New Hampshire native.

"I think it's a throwback to another time," he said, "back to the days when virtually every general store had a barrel of pickled tripe on hand. It didn't have to be tightly stored because the pickle juice would preserve it. That was important because up until the 1950s, a lot of people didn't have reliable refrigerators to store it.

"It *is* an acquired taste," he confessed, so, in my continuing effort to bring you all that is New Hampshire, I set off to Rosie's to find people who had acquired it.

I brought photographer Bob LaPree along for moral support.

Big mistake.

Waitress Shelley Byrne—she's Rosie's daughter—could not have been more accommodating. She even made Tony Sanchez-Young wait for her lunch, since she's a devout lover of fried tripe and Shelley knew that, while dining, she'd be willing to discuss her affliction.

Sorry. I meant "affection."

"I started eating it when I was a kid down Maine," Tony said. "We lived on a farm and we ate everything. Pheasant. Grouse. Tripe. And when we were cutting up the tripe, we'd eat pieces raw."

I don't know what turned first. My head or my stomach. And mine weren't the only parts turning.

"I've been working for my mother since 1972," Shelley said, "and I still won't touch it with my fingers. We have customers who swear by it. They come here from Maine and Massachusetts for it, but if I have to fix tripe, I use a fork."

Diner Carole Drouin weighed in from a booth nearby.

"I classify tripe with tongue," she said, "and I don't want anything to do with either of them. I just don't like the look of it. Raw or cooked, doesn't matter."

The batter matters to those who savor the fried tripe at Rosie's though. Cook Barbara Stevens applies just a light dusting before immersing the tripe into deep fat. When it floats to the surface, she knows it's done.

And it's the only way she knows.

She doesn't eat it either.

"I'm not that brave," she said. "I don't even eat cucumbers. I'll cook it all day long. I don't mind that at all, but I just can't bring myself to taste it."

I was firmly in Shelley's and Carole's and Barbara's camp on that one, only to find out that photographer Bob—heretofore my friend—had quietly asked her to throw in a side of fried tripe for us to share.

I felt like a tripe inspector.

You know, it was gut-check time.

I could back down and risk ridicule because, as a rule, I don't eat meat, but I tried to convince myself that tripe isn't *really* meat. It's like an organ. Innards. Entrails, really. Nothing but harmless, run of-the-mill, guts-and-gizzards kind of stuff.

I wasn't exactly winning myself over with *that* argument, but then

I figured, what the heck? People have eaten this stuff for centuries, and while many of those people are, in fact, dead, tripe is still popular with some of the survivors.

In many Middle Eastern countries, they eat a stuffed tripe called "Keebayat." In Syria, they eat a stuffed lamb tripe called "Gumee" and Italians enjoy a delicacy called "Trippa con fagioli," which sounds way more fancy than the English translation, which is "tripe with beans."

And what about tripe soup? I guess everybody eats tripe soup. In Sweden, it's "Busecca Ticinese." In Bulgaria, it's "Chkembe Tchorba." In the Czech Republic, it's "Drstkova Polevka" and in Mexico, it's called "Menudo" and, if it is eaten with plenty of hot peppers, it is reputed to cure hangovers.

And I felt like I had the sword of Damocles hanging over my head as I raised my tripe-filled fork to my lips. I turned to make sure photographer Bob was doing the same—my Momma didn't raise no dope—and then we were chewing in unison.

And chewing.

And chewing.

"Notice how you really get the pickling flavor on the back of your tongue?" Bob noted helpfully, as if that would keep me from stabbing him with my fork.

"Mmmm hmmm," I replied.

"And what about the texture?" he asked. "Notice the texture?"

"Mmmm hmmm," I replied.

I continued to grin foolishly, sitting at the counter with my mouth filled with tripe, when a song started running through my mind. It's a catchy little number by Little Feat. It's called "Tripe Face Boogie." I never knew what it meant before.

And now I was doing it.

Well, needless to say, I survived. Through sheer will power, I managed to avoid the ultimate gastronomic disaster, if you catch my drift, and when I got back to the office, after I removed Bob's phone number from my Rolodex, I called Steve Taylor (who got me into this in the first place) to bravely compare notes on the taste of tripe.

"I wouldn't know," he said. "I don't eat the stuff."

(11/19/98)

A Class of His Own

I know it's hard to work a baseball analogy in the dead of winter, but imagine pitching a no-hitter on the last day of the regular season, only to find that your team left your name off the World Series roster.

Now imagine being Kip Griffin.

At this very moment, he is the best aerial inverted freestyle skier in America—no, make that the world—yet he, like you and me, will be watching the 1998 Olympic Winter Games on television.

"Yeah, I'll probably be watching it at P.J. O'Sullivan's," he said. "Now that's not bad, but I wouldn't mind eating sushi in Nagano either."

They don't serve sushi at P.J.'s—that's his favorite watering hole in Manchester—but the menu doesn't matter. Whatever Kip orders, it's sure to be bittersweet, just like his victory in the 1998 FIS World Cup final at Breckenridge, Colorado, last Saturday.

For the record, his triumph in that final pre-Olympic World Cup event makes him the reigning champion in his chosen sport—it's like a cross between gymnastics and sky diving on skis—but it wasn't enough to overcome one simple fact.

It came a week too late.

An abbreviated qualifying schedule—one that was cut short by bad weather in both Europe and North America—left him decimal points short in the complex scoring system that would have locked him onto the U.S. Olympic team.

Still, there was hope. At the eleventh hour, officials from the U.S. Olympic Ski Team considered factoring in the results from Breckenridge. They didn't. So in the end, Kip could have captured the World Cup finale with a quad-twisting triple off Mount Olympus, and it wouldn't have meant a damn.

Most athletes would have flipped, but aerial inverted skiing great Kip Griffin from Bedford—the reigning World Cup champion—accepted his exclusion from the 1998 Olympic Ski Team with customary class. (Photo Courtesy of Kip Griffin)

Of course, with him, such a feat is not out of the question. He's done things on skis none of us would ever even attempt.

Well, not on purpose anyway.

Picture yourself careering down a steep, snow-covered ramp that curls up ominously at the end, all the better to hurl you into the air. Now, once you reach 40 miles per hour, imagine leaping from the crest of that ramp, thrusting your body even higher so you can begin a series of torques and twists and fully inverted turns before landing—ideally on your skis—on a slope that's pitched at 80 degrees.

Now do it again.

And again.

That's what the Bedford resident's been doing for the past eight years, ever since he abandoned soccer (he was a goalkeeper at Plymouth State College) and mogul skiing (he was an instructor at Loon Mountain) to pursue his Olympic dream.

But first, he had to get his feet wet.

Literally.

"It's called the 'aerial law,'" he explained. "Before you can even try a jump on the snow, you have to be qualified on water, so you have to perform the jump into the pool at least 100 times.

"Picture yourself standing on the side of a pool and falling into the water chest first," he said. "Now imagine doing the same thing from 30 feet in the air and hitting the water. Everyone winds up spitting blood now and then from the internal bruising."

All of that early training at Lake Placid paid off, however, because in a sport where they keep the ambulances running at the bottom of the hill, Kip Griffin remained remarkably healthy. At least until the 1996 U.S. Nationals at Park City, Utah.

"The weather was God awful," he said "The snow was like mashed potatoes, it was maybe 50 degrees and the jumps were falling apart. I shouldn't have jumped."

But he did.

"I've never seen the film," he said. "I know there are a lot of copies out there, but I've never seen it and I've never wanted to see it."

All of the circumstances—and perhaps a hint of hesitation on his part—left him out in front of his landing. As he touched down, his momentum threw him forward into an out-of-control tumble. When he finally came to a stop, all he could do was wait for the helicopter.

"They called off the competition after my run," he said. "They had to. They had to get the 'Life Flight' in to get me out. If you blow out your shoulder or your knee, they can walk you to a car, but when you do what I did to my leg . . ."

What he did to his left leg was shatter the femur, the long bone of the thigh. For the next year, a femoral rod and three screws held the bone together while he tried to rehab his body. In March of 1997, the hardware was surgically removed. Then it was time to rehab his psyche.

"It's the kind of sport where you spend six years convincing yourself you won't get hurt," he said, "and then it happens and you forget about the hundreds and hundreds of jumps you landed. You tell yourself you just want to jump and land safe, but you can't do that—and you can't win—until the day you stop thinking about it."

He was waiting for that day throughout the fall, as the World Cup tour wound through Europe.

"I knew I had to jump to get the skeletons out of my head," Kip said, so he toughed it out through World Cup stops like Tignes, France, and Piancavallo, Italy, but it wasn't until Jan. 2—when he was back at Lake Placid—that he knew he was back in business.

Clearly, he had the talent and the heart. What he didn't have was time and so, when he nailed his two jumps last Saturday—besting 51 other athletes from 26 nations, most of them Olympians—his time had already run out.

So now he is retired. His choice. Just like that. Unlike golf, however, there's no seniors tour for aerial inverted freestyle skiers, so, at the age 31, what does the future hold for Kip Griffin?

"It's hard to say," he said. "When you're thinking about the Olympics, there's such a focus that you don't spend a lot of time working on your backup plan. I'd like to be involved in sports commentary or marketing and promotion, maybe product design if anyone out there is looking"—he laughed, but he was serious—"and then there's the wedding."

Ah yes, the wedding. On Sept. 6, Kip will marry Chris Deschenes, but even on that joyous day, there will be an Olympian touch of irony. Mariano Ferrario, a close friend on the U.S. Ski team—one who will be at the Olympics—will be in his wedding party.

"Even he said to me that I should be going in his place," Kip said, "but I told him not to think that way. I told him to go out and prove everyone wrong. He's going to be a part of Chris's and my life forever."

You know, the crazy thing about it is, for all of his personal disappointment, Kip feels like he has somehow let *us* down.

"Of course you want it for yourself," he said, "but then you start thinking about your family and your friends and how so many people back home are pulling for you and then you realize that you want it for everyone else so bad. And then..."

And then he looks away.

A few years down the line, there will come a day when the rain and cold will make his leg ache. He'll probably wince, but hopefully, the ache will make him smile because it will remind him of the places he's been and the friends he's made and the things he's done and unlike the rest of us, he'll have the satisfaction of knowing what it feels like to be the best in the world.

Today, he *is* the best in the world.

And tonight, at P.J. O'Sullivan's, when the opening ceremonies of the 1998 Olympic Winter Games are on TV, he'd better have the best seat in the house.

(2/6/98)

Even when they're in the middle of a circle—like the one at this Plaistow dance class—Polly and Jim Floyd can still dance circles around the competition. (Union Leader Photo by Bob LaPree)

Tripping the Light Fantastic

STEP LIVELY NOW, FOLKS. This ain't no retirement home, so if you're going to keep up with Polly and Jim Floyd, you're going to have to be light on your feet.

And it doesn't matter if the good Lord blessed you with more than the normal complement of left feet, either. You're still welcome to toe the line with the rest of the line dancers who fill their classes throughout Southern New Hampshire.

So if it's Wednesday, this must be Plaistow, where 25 seniors have crowded onto the dance floor at the Vic Geary Drop-In Center. After laying out enough steps to make this Baryshnikov blanch, Polly cues up a 45-rpm—remember them?—then proceeds to walk and talk her pupils through their paces.

"There's some jazz boxes, a back box, a pair of scissors and a step-step cross," warned Polly, who—for those of us unschooled in the jargon of line dancing—might just as well have been speaking Swedish.

"The hardest part about this one is getting started to the music," she explained. "It only has one pick-up note, and if you miss it . . ."

Okay, so some of them missed the pick-up note, but nobody misses dance class when Jim and Polly come to town. Not that anyone here is bound for the Bolshoi, mind you.

"Most teachers? They're too damn serious," said Norman Ethier, 78, who crosses the Massachusetts state line to line dance with the Floyds. "They make it fun, and of all the classes you can go to, they make sure you get it right."

That's a universal sentiment amongst Jim and Polly's students, many of whom have seen line dance instructors employ the "march or die" philosophy. That doesn't sit right with these laid back seniors, even the ones who aren't all that "senior."

"I'm like the class clown," said Janet Bumpus of Kingston, who—at a mere 58—is the baby of this bunch. Which is not to imply that anyone here is "old." Old is a relative term when you're talking about a group that includes the Floyds.

Just because Jim is 84 and Polly is 82, hey, that doesn't mean they're old. And when it comes to tripping the light fantastic, they're just kids.

Why, they've been married for 64 years, but the Floyds didn't even take up dancing until 1964. That's when friends invited them for a little bit of square dancing in Derry with the group known as the "Space Town Squares."

After a few years of square dancing, they decided to knock the corners off and try their luck at round dancing. And given the Astro-theme tied to all things Derry in those days, it goes without saying that the round dancing troupe would be known as the "Orbits."

Get it?

Anyway, the round dancing held their attention for a time, but 10 years ago, when it was time to try a new step or two, the Floyds made the logical geometric progression from squares to rounds to lines.

Which brings us on a straight line back to Plaistow.

"Heel, heel, out to the front then cross," called Polly from the front of the line, as the sound of "All My Exes Live in Texas" filled the room. That, and the earnest shuffle of sneaker-clad feet on linoleum.

"My parents are 68 and 71 and they're old compared to those people," said Janis Milliken, who watched from the kitchen window as she prepared lunch for the seniors. "It's like they say. If you don't use it, you'll lose it, and that Polly's a hoot."

And there are plenty of hoots from the dancers when they finally coax Jim and Polly into the center of a circle. At every class in every town—be it Hampstead or Plaistow or Derry—the students beg their teachers to suspend the lessons at least once each session so they can strut their stuff. The Floyds oblige, gracefully, but sometimes begrudgingly, in Jim's case.

"I didn't start dancing till after I was 50," he explained. "I was too busy making a living before that, but dancing has been good to us. You could sit at home and deteriorate in front of the TV, but once you get out and the music gets going . . ."

The music has kept them going through cancer and heart attacks and cataracts and their latest hurdle, the macular degeneration that is claiming Jim's vision.

"But it only affects my reading and my driving," he smiled. "It doesn't affect my dancing."

So Polly does the driving these days. Three days a week, from their home in Brentwood, they load their gear into their 1988 Ford Tempo—turntable, speakers, tape deck, mixer and microphone—and set a tempo for everyone else to follow.

"Looking at them," said Janet Bumpus, "I'm not afraid to get old."

(10/7/97)

The waters of Rye Harbor are like a second home for Arthur Splaine, who's been lobstering off the New Hampshire coast for most of his life. (Union Leader Photo by John Clayton)

A Lobster in Every Pot

IT'S HARD TO MAKE any "Old Man and the Sea" references when you're writing about lobsterman Arthur Splaine. He's only 43, but even at that relatively tender age, he's already been catching crustaceans in the waters off Rye Harbor for more than 30 years.

That's a lotta lobster.

He got his first boat when he was 12 years old, a little 10-footer. When he was 15, he got a loan, bought another boat and went into business for himself.

"My aunt worked at the bank," explained Art, whose sense of humor may be the only thing that's dry at the end of his work day. "The only way to get a mooring was to buy someone's boat and business, so I did. It cost $2,500."

It was a prudent investment.

Back then, there was a 15-year wait for moorings in Rye Harbor. Now it's up to 20 years, and for a kid who grew up within a stone's throw of the inlet—okay, maybe two throws—that kind of wait was out of the question.

"You could see right away he was a kid with a passion for the water," said Leo Axtin, the harbormaster at Rye and proprietor of Granite State Whale Watch. "If you look around the harbor, you'll always find two or three kids who can't wait to get an outboard throttle in their hands. Art was one of them."

Leo still shakes his head at the boy's work ethic.

"When he was too young to work on a boat, he'd be here in the morning renting fishing gear to people," he said. "By the time he got his first boat, I think he had 21 lobster traps. People gave him some and he made the rest himself. When I finally hired him as a deck hand, he'd go out early and work his traps. By the time I'd get here in the morning, he'd be here waiting for me."

Back then, the traps were made of oak. Today, they're made of galvanized wire coated with plastic. Some things are still the same, however. Art still has the same nickname—"Squeak"—and he still has the same basic schedule, although these days, he has a few more traps to work. Say a thousand more.

"We do about a quarter of them every day," he said. "That way, by Friday, we're back to the traps we checked on Monday and we just keep the cycle going."

And checking the traps means more than just removing the lobster. It also means rebaiting them once the catch is retrieved, an extremely aromatic process involving half a dozen herring in mesh bags.

"You may not like the smell," he said, "but the lobster do."

While much of his trade is tried and true, there is room for innovation. When lobster are retrieved from Art's traps, they are measured and the keepers are quickly placed upright in short lengths of PVC piping. The result looks a little undignified—like a lobster signaling a touchdown—but it's functional.

"That makes it easier to band them," said Mike Kozlowski, a full-time social worker who frequently plays first mate to Squeak's skipper. "And when you band them, always do the big claw first. It's faster than the other one."

Mike wears gloves when he uses the plier-like device to slip the heavy rubber bands over the claws, but it's still important to pay attention. One slip and you're in the lobster's grip. The resulting commotion—equally undignified—is best described as "the lobster dance."

All of this activity takes place on board a boat called the *Sea Hag,* which—to anyone who ever saw a Popeye cartoon—is hardly a flattering image. Is the name intended, perhaps, to scare off sea monsters?

"I couldn't tell you," Art explained. "Lloyd Hughes named it. He's the guy I bought the boat from. There's just a superstition about changing names on a boat that you buy. I had a friend who renamed two of his boats, one flipped and sank and the other burned up. I guess it's just bad luck for the boat, so I stuck with it."

Just as he has stuck with his trade.

After so many years in the lobstering game, Art knows that it has its economic ironies—he has a wholesale business called "Catch of the Day"—but everything pretty much averages out. For instance, the price of lobster generally drops in July and August, when both the supply and the demand—fueled by tourism—is at its highest.

"We catch more this time of year," he said, "because this is when the lobster shed, and when they shed, they move closer to shore and they get more active because they need more food to replace their shells."

But don't the new, soft shells mean less meat?

"Yup," Art said. "When you can open the claw shell without using a cracker, you're probably not going to get a lot of meat in that claw. The best lobster comes early in the year, winter and spring. The shells are hard and full of meat, but those lobster are out deeper and they don't move around as much. That makes them harder to catch, which means they cost more, but when they cost more, you get more."

You get all that?

While Art understands the complexities of his work, it's the simplicity he loves the most. And you can forget about that solitude-of-the-sea stuff, too. He loves having folks on board—Marilyn Quayle was his favorite passenger-turned-deck-hand—and he handles questions like a seasoned teacher.

All things considered though, there's one thing he'd rather you not ask.

"Just don't ask me if I eat lobster," he laughed. "I'd never cook one for myself. If I eat them twice a year, it's only because we have folks over and they want them. My wife won't touch them. Neither will my daughter Colby. The only one in the family who likes them is my daughter Kelsey."

It makes sense. If you work at McDonald's all day, the last thing you want on your plate is a quarter pounder. Art feels the same way about pound-and-a-quarters. So if he isn't in the business for the lobster, why *is* he in it?

"Well, I enjoy the ocean, obviously, but more than anything else, it's the independence. I've had other jobs," (he has a degree in engineering) "but even when I worked, I still kept my traps. I like being my own boss and making my own decisions. I think it would be awful hard to work for somebody else now."

(8/6/98)

Frederick Teague and his fellow members of Le Grande Voiture 40 & 8 have kept their promise to preserve the Merci Box Car in West Manchester. (Union Leader Photo by Bob LaPree)

The Merci Box Car

THEY'VE BEEN DOING THIS for nearly 50 years now, but as usual, there were curious looks and puzzled glances as the dignified men *of Le Grande Voiture 40 & 8* paraded down Bremer Street on Manchester's West Side yesterday.

Their destination?

The Merci Box Car.

Tucked away on a short, dead-end stretch of Reed Street, this extraordinary—some would say unusual—token of affection from the people of France is an often overlooked piece of history. Overlooked, that is, by all but the members of the 40 & 8, the veterans fraternal organization whose members long ago vowed to preserve the rail car, and its significance, for future generations.

And so they convened again yesterday, as they do on the second Sunday of every October, to remember their fallen comrades—"the Voyageurs"—who have passed away since last they gathered here.

The procession was a grand one, some 150 strong. The pageantry was provided by the American Legion Band from Keene's Gordon Bissell Post and the women's auxiliary and a host of uniformed color guards from throughout New Hampshire, all of whom gathered outside the brick and glass pavilion that houses the box car.

But what is it about this old gray railroad car, now empty, that fills it with such significance? Why have men like Fred Teague and the late Donald Still invested so much time and energy toward its preservation?

To know that, one must go back to 1947, a time when the people of America came to the aid of France. Not as military allies, this time, but as friends of the embattled French people.

Even two years after the end of World War II, food and clothing were in short supply throughout much of Europe, so the American people, with prodding from newspaper columnist Drew Pearson, responded by sending a 700-car "Friendship Train," laden with relief supplies, to the people of France.

In return, the people of France responded with a symbolic train of their own, a "Thank You Train"—hence the *Merci* Box Car. As the train traveled though the towns and villages and provinces of France, citizens were encouraged to fill the tiny cars with personal mementos and artwork and photographs and letters and other tokens of gratitude for the people of America.

The response? More than 250 tons of "gratitude" filled the train by the time it reached port at Le Havre, and an additional 9,000 gifts had to be left behind when the French cargo ship Magellan departed for New York Harbor.

When it docked on Feb. 3, 1949, the ship carried 49 box cars, one for each of the 48 states and one to be shared by the District of Columbia and the territory of Hawaii.

The odd-looking cars were not unfamiliar to American servicemen. Long before they became links in a gift to America, the 40 & 8 boxcars had a special place—for better or worse—in the hearts of American fighting men.

During World War I, most khaki-clad doughboys bound for France reached their American port of departure on roomy Pullman sleeper cars. Once in France, however, their journey to the front lines frequently came in the tiny 40 & 8 boxcars.

The origin of the name? It's simple enough. It's based upon the capacity of the box car itself. In transporting men and materiel to battle, the cars were capable of carrying 40 men or eight horses.

In French, that's *"Quarante Hommes et Huit Chevaux."*

Understandably, the Yanks were either amused or repulsed by their means of transit, and then there was the sergeant who, as they say, got lost in the translation. "I got all my 40 artillery-men in the box car," he told his lieutenant, "but if you try to put eight of our horses in, somebody's gonna be trampled to death."

Experiences like that—for better or worse—formed the basis, in 1920, for the good-natured formation of the 40 & 8, the "fun" American Legion subsidiary known formally as *"La Societe des Quarante Hommes et Huit Chevaux."*

And, some 29 years down the line, who better to take responsibility for the box car than the organization that took it as its *raison d'être?* In New Hampshire, it made perfect sense, and for those of us who care about such things, there could not have been a better choice.

As proof, consider the unfortunate outcome in other states where the Merci Box Cars have been subjected to varying indignities down through the years.

In Idaho, for instance, the historic box car is situated at the Idaho Penitentiary in Boise, hardly a reminder of international friendship. In Nebraska, the gift from the French people was sold for scrap. Sale price? Forty-five bucks. In other states—like Connecticut, Rhode Island and New Jersey—the cars were destroyed by fire.

In still other states, the cars are dying from benign neglect, something the Grand Voiture of New Hampshire vowed would never happen here.

"I didn't get to see it the day it arrived in New Hampshire, but I remember when it got here," said Teague, 71, a Navy veteran and retired carpenter who serves as volunteer caretaker for the box car and the pavilion in which it sits.

It's a responsibility he takes to heart.

"I feel it's part of the heritage of this country," he said, "and someone has to keep it up. I know a lot of people have forgotten why it came here in the first place, and I just wish we could make it so more people knew what it stood for."

It's hard to tell how many folks remember the day the box car first arrived in Manchester. It was Feb. 10, 1949. Thousands gathered at Elm and Market streets outside City Hall to see the car, adorned as it was—and still is—with the colorful coats-of-arms of the 20 French provinces.

Its treasures, in accordance with the wishes of the French people, have since been scattered amongst the schools and libraries and veterans organizations of the state. All that remains in the box car itself is a single bronze vase, a gift from one Monsieur Lavertu from *"le Bibliotheque, Ville de Cherbourg."*

The greatest treasure? That's still the box car itself. That, and the members of *Le Grande Voiture* 40 & 8 who, true to their word, have kept it for all to see.

(10/13/97)

Even now, more than 40 years after the publication of "Peyton Place" earned her national renown, Grace Metalious is still a mystery to many in her hometown. (Larry Smith Photo Courtesy of the New Hampshire Historical Society)

Grace Under Pressure

TELL ME IF THIS SOUNDS FAMILIAR: A bright young writer from Manchester—homely, but not unattractive—a free spirit with working class roots who likes to wear jeans and sneakers (and also enjoys an occasional touch of the grape) writes a shockingly successful first book that tickles some and offends others en route to making the author a household name.

Me? Yeah, right. I'm not even a household name in my own household.

No, I'm talking about Grace (DeRepentigny) Metalious, the Manchester native whose first novel was like a fingernail on the chalkboard of America's social consciousness nearly 40 years ago.

Perhaps you've heard of it.

It was called *Peyton Place.*

Critics called it "crude," "immoral," "vulgar" and "senseless," but remember—God's honest truth—those are precisely the words Leo Tolstoy used to describe William Shakespeare.

Besides, that kind of critical language may make authors cringe but it makes publicists salivate, and thanks to the clever exploitation of that Puritanical outcry, Grace's hard-bitten, soft-core assault on small-minded, small-town America became the most successful first novel in publishing history.

Within 10 days of its publication in 1955, more than 60,000 hardcover copies of *Peyton Place* had been sold. Since then, more than 10 million copies have been put into print, including editions in French, German and Spanish, not to mention Italian, Japanese, Danish, Norwegian, Swedish and yes, even Yiddish. (That Allison MacKenzie, what a *mensch*).

Not bad for a kid right out of the Manchester neighborhood

called Janesville, a graduate of the Ash Street School who went on to flunk English as a sophomore at Central High School.

Understandably, a lot of folks around here are unaware of Grace's ties to Manchester. It's not like there's a school or a park named in her honor. Nonetheless, her writing roots were firmly planted in the soil of this city, even if it has yielded rather a bitter harvest.

"I don't know that we'll ever see a Grace Metalious Park in Manchester," said historian Robert Perreault, who will conduct a seminar on *Peyton Place* at the Carpenter Memorial Library Thursday night. "This city has enough trouble honoring its own history, so I wouldn't hold my breath waiting for it to honor an author who provokes thought, even when she's one of our own."

Bob's interest in Grace Metalious is a matter of scholarly record. In addition to his published works regarding her French-Canadian ancestry—her given name was Grace Marie Antoinette Jeanne d' Arc de Repentigny—and its influence on her writing, he's also conducted walking tours past the various homes and apartments where she lived in the city.

"For me, she's like a hometown hero," he said. "I know a lot of people don't see it that way, but I think she deserves a second chance.

"She and her book just got caught up in the sensationalism of the day, but now that the dust has settled, I say let's go back and read the book. It's a fine piece of writing."

Unfortunately, a series of events—including one flip remark by the author—hoisted it beyond the realm of literature and into the category of social phenomenon.

Just as *Peyton Place* was about to be released, Grace's publisher hired a hustling publicist whose previous clients included literary giants like Captain Kangaroo. When he brought Associated Press columnist Hal Boyle to visit Grace's Gilmanton home, she joked that her husband—fellow Manchester native George Metalious—would probably lose his job as principal of the local high school because of the book.

Sure enough, by the time Boyle's column ran, that off-hand remark was written as fact. In fact, it became a self-fulfilling prophecy, and even without scandal sheets like the *National Enquirer* or tabloid TV shows like "Hard Copy," the racy *Peyton Place* caught fire.

It didn't hurt that Grace was occasionally, um ... ungracious.

"To tourists, these towns look as peaceful as a postcard," she told Boyle. "But if you go beneath that picture, it's like turning over a rock with your foot. All kinds of strange things crawl out."

She bristled when asked if the book was autobiographical. One interviewer had the audacity to pose the question on TV—ever hear of Mike Wallace?—so she retaliated by calling him Myron (he hates his given name) and asking him how many times he had been married.

Under the withering glare of the spotlight, Grace hit the bottle harder than ever. Her subsequent work suffered accordingly, but within the next 10 years, she cranked out a sequel to *Peyton Place* and two other novels—*The Tight White Collar* and *No Adam in Eden*—the last of which holds particular ties to Manchester.

"It's probably the least known of her four books, and it is depressing," explained Bob Perreault, "but there's so much local color that I thought it was delightful. If you know Manchester, you can read that book and identify everything she's talking about."

This week, at least, people will be talking about her.

The New Hampshire Humanities Council—as part of a program entitled "What New Hampshire Is Reading"—is sponsoring a series of discussions around the state on *Peyton Place.* So why are Granite Staters reading a 40-year-old novel? That's what I asked program coordinator Debbie Watrous.

"For one thing, it fits well in the context of our whole project which is to study New Hampshire voices, different ways of looking at who we are in this state," she said. "It started last month with *Our Town* by Thornton Wilder which was a very nice view of small town life. I think it's safe to say that Grace Metalious had a totally opposite view.

"I'm not going to say it's great literature, but it is a good book, and a lot of people don't know that because of the firestorm when it was published," Debbie added. "I think it's interesting to see what she was saying about the human condition from her point of view, what she was saying about men and women, about the wealthy and underclass and rape and incest and alcoholism and things people didn't talk about in the 1950s."

Everybody but Grace, that is. She talked about it, she wrote about it and she paid a price. She died a tragically premature death in 1964 at the age of 39 due to alcohol-related ailments, having squandered—for the most part—her fortune and her talent.

But now she is being resurrected, if only for a short time, in the city of her birth. So take a chance. Read the book—adults only please—then join in the discussion and recognize the achievements of this remarkable woman.

Just do me one favor. Try and ignore the part about the gossipy neighborhood know-it-all named Clayton. If you don't mind.

(10/31/94)

Adam Sandler movies may puzzle older filmgoers, but younger ones—like Shawn Moses, left, and Sam McGowen—have made the Manchester comedian a matinee idol. (Union Leader Photo by David Burroughs)

Star Gazing

I HAVE A CONFESSION to make. I've been to three Adam Sandler movies in my life, and in each case, I was paid to attend.

Thus far, I wouldn't have it any other way.

Nothing against Adam, mind you. He's a Manchester guy, I'm a Manchester guy and we have a lot of mutual friends and these mutual friends are always telling me how hilarious he is which just proves . . . well, which proves nothing.

When it comes to Adam Sandler movies, I just don't get it.

I *want* to get it. I really do. No one is a bigger fan of "local boy makes good" stories than I am and commercially speaking, Adam Sandler is, without question, the single most successful entertainer ever to come out of New Hampshire.

His numbers are staggering.

After winning his spurs on NBC's "Saturday Night Live,", he got supporting roles in films like *Airheads* and *Mixed Nuts*. Then he landed a starring role in *Billy Madison*, portraying a sensitive-but-angry illiterate heir to a family fortune who falls in love with his remedial grade school teacher. The critics savaged it.

It grossed $25.5 million.

Then he starred in *Happy Gilmore* as a sensitive-but-angry hockey player trying to make it on the pro golf tour in order to rescue his grandmother's house from IRS foreclosure. The critics ravaged it.

It grossed $40 million at the box office and $35 million more on video.

Now comes his latest film entitled *The Wedding Singer.* Hold on to your hats. If not for the titanic take of *Titanic*, *The Wedding Singer* would be the highest grossing movie in America. In the first 10 days after its release, the movie raked in $39 million, and that's not counting the gate from Tuesday's matinee at Hoyt's Cinema on South Willow Street. That's where I watched the film, along with about 40 other, um, *cine fanatiques.*

Some were restless with anticipation.

"I plan on laughing very hard," said Dave Michaud, 19, who admitted that he was "really into" Adam Sandler. He proved it by quoting the following humorous line from *Happy Gilmore*: "You're going to get it, Bobby."

I guess you had to be there.

Mike Duarte was. He's 18.

"*Happy Gilmore* was my favorite," Mike agreed.

Then there was Jeff Goldberg, who's 14. He didn't bring his Adam Sandler CDs along, but he did bring his father, Joel Goldberg, who looked slightly uncomfortable.

"He's more of a fan than I am," Joel said, nodding toward his son.

Then the lights went down. For the next 96 minutes, we were all awash in *The Wedding Singer,* a film that was short on laughs but long on songs, really bad songs from the 80s—Culture Club, Thompson Twins, Madonna—a techno-decade of music that almost makes you pine for the depth and complexity of disco.

Now I'm not a movie critic, but I played one on TV—seriously—and if I had to describe my feelings about *The Wedding Singer* in a single word, the word would be "mixed." I am not alone. The film industry is seriously divided about this movie.

Roger Ebert (thumbs down) from the *Chicago Sun-Times* said the film was further evidence of the "dumbing down" of America, while Kevin Thomas of the *Los Angeles Times* called it "a sparkling romantic comedy" and *Mademoiselle* magazine's Anne Marie O'Connor—who is either on drugs or on the payroll of New Line Cinema—said it was a "screamingly funny 80s flashback."

Of course, the truth probably lies somewhere in the middle, and Janet Maslin of the *New York Times* staked out that middle ground fairly well when she said the film "had enough enjoyable silliness to please Mr. Sandler's fans (but) avoids the mean-spirited humor" that colored *Billy Madison* and *Happy Gilmore.*

So where does this field of divided opinion leave us? If I may borrow a phrase from another recent film title, I am dazed and confused.

While producers bill the film as a "romantic comedy," the romance was lame and the comedy was absent. As the romantic lead, Adam dramatically underplays his role, which is a drastic departure from the demented frat-boy overacting that made his first two starring roles so annoying.

And just so you know, it's not that I have a problem with so-called "goon humor" either. When I saw *Dumb & Dumber,* I laughed so hard at one particular scene—I'm thinking "Turbo-Lax"—that I flat-out embarrassed myself. Now *Dumb & Dumber* isn't exactly what you'd call high-brow, Noel Coward-type humor, but geez, compared to *Billy Madison,* it's like *Citizen Kane.*

Anyway, I keep telling myself that it's me.

I keep telling myself that maybe Adam Sandler is in the midst of a Jerry Lewis thing. Maybe one day, the people of France will present him with the Legion of Honor and I'll realize what a fool I was to have overlooked this genius in our midst.

In the meantime, while I wait for him to deliver a cohesive, breakthrough, tour-de-force performance that might put him in the comedic realm of say, a Steve Martin or even a Dennis Leary, I'm sure Adam's laughing all the way to the bank.

And I couldn't be happier for him if I was, well . . . if I was Happy Gilmore.

I just wish I got it.

(2/27/98)

The naturalization services held regularly at the federal courthouse in Concord provide a nice reminder of New Hampshire's immigrant heritage. (Union Leader Photo by George Naum)

The Immigrants

FUNNY, THEY DIDN'T LOOK like huddled masses. You didn't get the sense that they were the wretched refuse of any teeming shores either. They were just folks—albeit folks from the four corners of the Earth—who wanted something we all take for granted.

They wanted to be Americans.

And so they gathered in the fifth floor courthouse in the federal building in Concord yesterday, 67 of them, to raise their hands and renounce "allegiance and fidelity" to any foreign princes or potentates.

We're not big on potentates around here.

This naturalization ritual's been done before. There's a solemnity and a dignity, but it never loses its essential joy. The clerks smile. The Elks hand out American flags. The men and women from the American Legion shake hands and get misty, God bless 'em, just like their new countrymen.

Alexander Graham Bell did this. So did Irving Berlin and Joseph Pulitzer and Samuel Gompers and Knute Rockne and yesterday, just like those men that went before him, Albert Sackey did it, too.

Freedom. Sometimes it's hard to wrap your mind around a notion as abstract as freedom. For us, it's a constant. It's a given. It's like the sun and the sky. It's always been there. Always will be, right?

Albert Sackey knows better.

He's from Ghana. Fifteen years ago, he was on the fast track (if there is such a thing) in that West African nation. He was serving his country, working in the office of the president. Then an upstart decided it was time for a change in government.

Not an election. A military coup.

The notion of freedom suddenly became far less abstract for Albert.

"If I was lucky, I would have spent the rest of my life in prison," he said. And if he wasn't lucky?

"I would have been dead."

So he fled. He was exiled. He spent time in refugee camps and made his way to the coast and hung on until he was able to make passage to the United States. He settled in Somersworth. Now, at 40, he works as a welder.

"It's good work," he said. "Honest work."

For 15 years, he was a man without a country. Not anymore.

For Albert Sackey, it was politics. For Saijan Singh Bhangoo, it was religion. In the Punjab region of India—the ancient home of the Sikhs—members of his faith are persecuted without mercy. In 1984, soldiers from the Indian government attacked a non-violent protest at their holiest shrine. More than 3,000 died.

After setting up a human rights watch in Canada, Saijin came to the United States. He lives in Hampstead when he isn't in Washington, D.C. He's the executive director of the World Sikh Organization.

"In India, the Sikhs are not free," he said. "My father still lives in India. He is 93 years old, and I cannot go and visit him. Here, there are no restrictions on how we practice our religion. In New Hampshire our motto is 'Live Free or Die.' For us, that is perfect."

You know what else is perfect? Mario Beaurivage is now an American citizen. He lives in Pelham. He's going to fit right in around here.

"I pay a lot of taxes here," he said, the lilt of his native Sherbrooke still evident in his voice. "I pay $5,000 in taxes on my house. I want to have my word to say about taxes. I want to vote."

Look for him at the next town meeting.

They don't get to vote much in Haiti, so you can bet that Luce Duvert will be casting a ballot in Manchester on Feb. 20. Down in Nashua, Abdolreza Shahabi will do the same, but make sure you call him Alex.

"I changed my name," said the Iranian native who has lived in America for 16 years, a period that coincides—not coincidentally—with the ascendance of the Ayatollah Khomeini.

"But for all of that time, I haven't been able to vote," he said. "I want to vote."

When Judge James Muirhead congratulated his fellow citizens, he reminded them that they were not alone. We are, after all, a nation of immigrants.

"One of the great strengths of this country," he said, "has always been the way we contribute our diverse backgrounds, share them with each other and become better and stronger for it."

It's nice to be reminded once in a while.

(1/27/96)

As long as Bill Williams is behind the counter at Williams' Store—and he's been there for more than 50 years—folks in Hillsborough know that all is right with the world. (Union Leader Photo by Dick Morin)

The General Store

BILL WILLIAMS PLACED the hot dogs on the old Stimpson meat scale. As he waited for the dial to settle on the gleaming white enamel unit, he couldn't help but think back on how such a time-tested machine had come to reside in his store.

"I bought this I don't know how many years ago," he said. "An old store up in Newport went out of business. Guess I should have a digital one by now."

We can only hope he was joking.

Putting a digital scale in Williams' Store would be like painting Ray Bans on the Mona Lisa. You just don't mess with the classics.

For more than a hundred years, the small store has been a beacon by the side of the road, provided, of course, you were on the winding road that runs from Hillsborough to Hillsborough Upper Village. Today—almost 50 years to the day since Bill Williams assumed ownership—it remains just that.

Don't look for any wild anniversary celebrations, though.

"I thought, about it," Bill laughed. "Maybe roll the prices back to 50 years ago on Saturday but to tell you the truth, I don't even remember what I paid for the store. My wife and I always disagreed. I say it was $5,500 and she always said $6,500."

It's an argument he'd love to have again, but his wife Ruth passed away 10 years ago. Maybe that's why, at 87, he still works in the store every day. They spent so much time there together, it's like she's still there.

"She used to get after me to sell the store," he smiled, "and I told her, 'You'll be sorry, having me around under foot all the time,' so that's why I never sold it.

"Besides," he asked, "what else would I do now? It's so easy to sit back and do nothing. That I don't want to do. I figure you can rust away or wear away. I'd rather wear away."

But Bill Williams wears well. There's a sense of calm, a gentleness, a serenity to the man, even when he's trading good-natured barbs with regulars like Doug Pelletier and Louis Iadonisi.

"The first time I came in here, he said, 'In God we trust. All others pay cash,'" said Louis, as he tucked copies of *The Union Leader* and *Boston Globe* under his arm.

"And I told him he didn't look like God," Bill laughed. "Besides, he's another flatlander."

Not that he's casting aspersions. Bill's a flatlander, too. When the war ended—that would be World War II—he found himself in New Jersey, but he didn't like his young wife commuting into New York City to work. They decided to look for something different.

"We were looking in real estate books for places in Virginia, Pennsylvania and New York state, maybe one of those little camps with overnight cabins, and then we saw a little store on the cover of one of those books. It said to contact the West Farm Agency, so we did. Then we drove out here and asked if we could see the store and the man—his name was Mr. Eaton—he said, 'Sure. Let's walk across the street.' And here we were."

When they closed the deal in June of 1948, Bill and Ruth moved upstairs over the store. They lived there for 13 years. It got to be a little tight, what with the gradual arrival of their four children, but Bill's never had a problem being around kids.

Why, you couldn't even count the number of kids who've stopped in over the years. Chances are anyone in town who's under the age of 50 has probably peered up over the edge of the same worn counter, only to find Bill Williams proffering a free pretzel stick.

It's been a rite of passage around Hillsborough.

It still is.

"Now when they come in, I give them a bag for their penny candy and let them fill it themselves," he smiled. "That's how a lot of 'em learn to count. And they're pretty good too. Well, at least I think they are."

Bill doesn't count the candy. He still runs his store on the honor system. That means he trusts the kids. Grown-ups too. That's why he doesn't make anyone sign for anything when they're short on cash.

"I never saw the point," he explained. "If their word's no good, their signature's no good. They pay me when they get to it. Or when

I get to it. I'm not real good about sending out bills, but people remember."

And when people remember Bill Williams, they do so fondly.

"He's the living image of the neighborhood grocer who cares about his customers," said Marcia Leizure, who runs the Parkside Gallery just down Route 31. "I remember being stuck at home in a snowstorm with my baby, and he'd always find someone to deliver milk to me. He'd say to another customer 'Hey, when you drive by Marcia's house, can you drop off this milk?' Who else would do that today?"

Today. Yesterday. All of the days have tended to blend into one over the years, leaving Bill Williams with a kind of career continuum.

"But lately," he said, "I've been slowing down."

Right. Slowing down. He's down to eight hours a day now. Still, he's entitled to slow down a little. In the early years, he never had the chance.

Back before he could persuade trucks to make deliveries to the store, he'd drive all over New Hampshire for merchandise to stock his shelves. One day he'd go to Keene for hardware from Spencer's. Then to Concord for groceries from C.A. King. Then to Manchester to buy wholesale from Varick's.

"When we lived in New York, we used to hear Italian in the city," he said, "but I remember the first time we went into Manchester. We were on Elm Street. My wife gave me this look. It seemed like everyone in the city was talking French."

It's funny to hear Bill Williams talk about all the things that have changed over the past 50 years. To sit in his store and pass the time of day, you'd think that nothing had ever changed.

And while you're there—as long as Bill Williams is there—nothing has.

(6/4/98)

Artist Bob Montana never lost the sense of joy, wonder and absurdity that is high school, which helps explain why "Archie" is among the best-selling comic books in history. (Photo Courtesy of Lynn Montana)

Back to the Drawing Board

When I was a kid—and please remember how much I love New Hampshire—I harbored a secret wish that one day my family would move to Riverdale.

I wanted to hang out with Archie.

You know, Archie Andrews, like in the comic book.

Yes, Archie, that eternally boyish, perpetual high school junior who proved on a daily basis that Riverdale was better than a male Fantasy Island in that the women there—Betty and Veronica in particular—actually fought over the men.

(For the record—and this is a pivotal, soul-baring, "either-or" choice that provides more definitive insight into the individual male psyche than any Rorschach test could ever reveal—I would have chosen Betty.)

All the better that this idyllic village of Riverdale was the vision of Bob Montana, the Manchester Central High School graduate (1940A) who never lost the ability to convey the sense of joy and wonder—and absurdity—that is high school.

"To me, Bob Montana and 'Archie' are Manchester's best-kept secrets," said syndicated cartoonist Larry White.

If so, the secret will be out on Thursday. That's when the Manchester Historic Association will hold a commemorative presentation on Montana's work, including original strips, early samples of his drawings and a discussion featuring White and long-time Montana collaborator, Jeff Cuddy.

"It was really a great privilege to work with him," Cuddy said, "because he taught me everything I know about comics. When I was learning his technique, I would stand at his shoulder and watch him and he was just *so deft.* He could just make those characters come alive."

In many ways, they are *still* alive.

So pervasive is the "Archie" influence in America that in the formative years of our most cutting-edge source of information, the Internet, programmers came up with a tool for searching archives.

Naturally, they named it "Archie."

Just last September, Archie and Veronica (that *vixen!*) wound up on the cover of "Yahoo," a leading Internet magazine and now comes word that filmmaker Tommy O'Haver—a big hit at the most recent Sundance Film Festival—is set to write and direct a musical comedy based on Archie & Company.

Not bad for characters who've been around since 1941.

That's when they were first liberated from Montana's imagination. With an alleged nudge from MLJ publisher John Goldwater, Bob's vision of the typical American teenager made a near-simultaneous debut in two comic books—"Pep" (# 22) and "Jackpot" (#4) for you collectors out there—and by the fall of 1942, the comic book had Archie's name on top.

Of course, by that time, Montana was serving with the U.S. Army Signal Corps. Upon his discharge in 1946, at the behest of King Features Syndicate, he moved "Archie" from comic book to newspaper strip—the reverse of the normal order—on the road to global renown.

At its peak, "Archie" appeared in more than 700 newspapers worldwide, and that's not counting the proliferation of comic book spin-offs like "Archie's Joke Book," "Archie's Pal, Jughead," "Archie's Girls, Betty and Veronica" and so on and so on.

"Since it caught hold, 'Archie' has been the largest selling non-super hero comic in the world," said White. "It's always been a good, clean comic that's been safe for the kids, but adults enjoyed it so much they even came but with a series of miniature books so it wouldn't look like they were reading comic books."

Such concern for appearances would not have troubled Montana, who was delightfully non-conformist. Perhaps that's to be expected from a man who—as the son of traveling vaudevillians—was born in a proverbial footlocker. His mom was a Ziegfeld girl named Roberta Pandolfini and his father was a banjo player named Ray Coleman who took, as his stage name, "The Great Montana."

The name stuck with the son.

So did the entertainer's mind set.

And when fate brought him to Manchester from Haverhill, Massachusetts, the Granite State simply became the confluence for rivers of talent and timing.

Naturally, such genius cannot function in a vacuum. Once established in the post-war era, Montana settled in Meredith, but his palette was continually enriched by family globetrotting. Prolonged stays in Mexico and Spain and Italy provided him with fresh ideas for the strip, as did the family itself.

"He had four children," said Cuddy, "and he told them, anyone who has an idea, put it on the refrigerator and I'll give you a quarter."

Certainly Montana struck a more lucrative arrangement with his assistant, Ruth Harding, the Maine native who not only lettered the strip, but offered situations and notions for the characters that Montana would then flesh out.

By 1962—after creating an "Archie" mural in the Manchester eatery called the Deli-Rama that delighted Montana—Cuddy was added to the mix as an inker and finish artist. That threesome thrived until Montana's sudden death—he suffered a heart attack while cross-country skiing at the age of 55—in 1975.

In an effort to keep the strip in New Hampshire, Cuddy picked up the mantle, but after a few weeks, he graciously bowed out.

"Bob was a genius," he said. "I couldn't keep up."

Who could? Over the years, the demands of this demanding trade have grown exponentially. With "Garfield" creator Jim Davis now presiding over a team of 35 artists and writers, one can only marvel at Montana's singular ability to create such a memorable stable of characters.

Bet you still remember them.

In addition to the headliners we've already mentioned, there's the oleaginous Reggie Mantle, lunkhead Moose Mason, goofy Big Ethel Muggs, the crotchety Miss Grundy, the buffoonish and balloonish principal Mr. Weatherbee and who could forget that prototypical cafeteria crone, Miss Beazly?

(Just to prove no good deed goes unpunished, when the American Society of Dietitians begged Montana to replace Miss Beazly with a more attractive character, he complied. He was then besieged by readers who wanted him to restore his less-than-comely creation. Eventually, he bowed to the wishes of the majority).

In the end, however—at least in these parts—Bob Montana's most enduring creation may have been Bob Montana himself.

(3/30/98)

The wilds of the North Country made an idyllic home for the family of forest ranger Alva Richardson, whose daughter became known as the "White Mountain National Forest Baby." (Union Leader Photo Illustration by Bob LaPree)

A Babe in the Woods

SEEING AS HOW she's going to be 70 years old tomorrow, it wouldn't seem fitting to call Betty (Richardson) McKenzie a babe in the woods.

But that's what she was.

The fact is, here in New Hampshire, she was the original babe in the woods. The "White Mountain National Forest Baby." That's what the newspapers called her when she was born back in 1927.

The proof is in the Berlin-Kilkenny range of the White Mountain National Forest. What with the arrival of hiking season, folks will be heading up this way and into those woods, and sooner or later, as they make their way around York Pond, those hardy souls may find themselves wading across Betty Brook.

It's Betty McKenzie's brook.

"I do remember my folks saying they wished they'd named a bigger brook after me," she recalled, "but that was the only one available."

Brooks weren't the only thing in short supply back then. There weren't many doctors around either, so Betty's father, one of the youngest men in the employ of the National Forest Service, sort of coached and coaxed his young wife through the birthing process, a process that took place in the tiny kitchen of a three-room guard station hard by the Wild River.

That was home to Alva and Mildred Richardson.

The particulars of Betty's arrival are recorded in a remarkable remembrance, a diary of life in the wilderness penned by her mother.

How else would Betty know that she was wrapped in cotton flannel bed sheets when she was born? Or that the doctor, upon his belated arrival, accidentally set his medical bag on top of her? Or that her birth was witnessed by as many as a hundred owls that had gathered outside the small cottage?

There's a *Little House on the Prairie* quality to the memoirs, as her mother's written reminiscences bring to life a spartan existence offset by the simple joys of love and devotion. She writes of commitment to work and to family, and in between the lines, she acknowledges the value of common sense in the wilderness and the consequences awaiting those who lack it.

Consider the unprepared tinhorns whose trips to the mountains were cut short by the black flies and "minges"—sometimes we call them "no-seeums"—that could drive a lesser man to distraction. Not little Betty, who, even as an infant, made every hike with her folks.

"We would put Betty in a knapsack with something in the bottom so she would not be too far down," her mother noted. "Her head was always out, and she seemed to love being out as much as I did. There wasn't much exposed on her except her head, and on that, I tied a kerchief with citronella rubbed on it and that seemed to do a pretty good job of keeping the pests away."

Would one expect less from the White Mountain National Forest Baby?

Hardly.

Even today, Betty—who prefers her given name of Beth—still marvels at the pluck of her parents, pluck that was demonstrated during her father's stint as a forest guard at the East Branch District near Jackson during the early 1920s.

"We had no refrigeration," Mildred wrote, "so all the perishables were put in sealed jars and suspended in the cool water in the stream in back of the camp. We were careful to attach a stout string to the jars and anchor them to a tree or a bush on the bank so they would not wash away or the raccoons get to them.

"We did not have fresh meat as often as we would have liked," she added. "In spite of the fact that I seared steak before putting it in a jar and in the cool water, it would not keep more than a couple of days."

Rather than settling for canned goods, however, the Richardsons learned to live off nature's bounty, be it spring water or brook trout or berries "bigger than the tip of a grown man's thumb."

Or—Ssssh!—moonshine.

"Al was very fond of home brew and a whiz at making it," Mildred confessed in her memoirs.

"He used to put it in the cold water of the bog near the house and it kept nearly as cold as a refrigerator would have kept it. He would put in raisins and prunes, anything he thought would taste good—even canned peaches—and it was supposed to be out of this world."

And it was another world the Richardson's occupied through Al's many postings, a world of trail building and fire towers and river crossings and Disney-like encounters with creatures in the wild. It was a world of quiet and solitude interrupted by the occasional logger or eccentric hiker and it was a world where big-city shopping meant an arduous hike into North Conway for provisions and maybe, just maybe, a night on the town.

"Going to the movies at North Conway was a treat I will always remember," Mildred wrote. "There was a small band that played before the movie would start and during the intervals. The conductor, who stood with his back to the audience, had a bald head on top, but around the sides, a wreath-like effect of thick curly hair.

"The poor man never had a chance," she added. "His bald spot was bombarded by the popcorn eaters. There must have been quite a heap of popcorn where he stood by the time the movie was over. He must have been used to it, because he never once faltered but kept right on conducting in spite of it all."

By today's standards, Alva and Mildred Richardson had little in the way of material possessions, but during their years together in the White Mountains—years when Mildred bore their three children, all told—they showed they possessed the kind of pioneering spirit required of his chosen profession.

As time has passed, so have most of the old-timers who knew Beth's folks and the life they lived.

Even the signs that once marked Betty Brook have disappeared through the years, which is why a recent note from the U.S. Geological Survey (based in Reston, Virginia) brought such joy to Betty's own daughter, Caroleen Dudley.

Just last month, Betty Brook was officially added to the U.S. Geographic Names Information System. It's a minor distinction, really, but a distinction that means the Richardsons' legacy—just like the brook that was named for a babe in the woods—will run on forever.

(6/19/97)

If someone doesn't come up with the money, plans to bring a bronze statue of Benjamin Franklin Keith back to New Hampshire may just go bust. (Photo Courtesy of Fred McLennan)

Vaudeville or Bust

WHEN THE TOPIC of "busts" comes up in show business circles, people tend to think of two things. Okay, three things.

One school of thought runs to bosomy stars like the late Jayne Mansfield—if you're counting along at home, that takes care of two of the things—while the other type of bust involves big-budget, motion picture flops.

Think of Elizabeth Taylor's *Cleopatra* or Warren Beatty's *Ishtar* or Kevin Costner's *The Postman* (which, take my word for it, you should avoid at all costs).

Then there is Fred McLennan.

He has another kind of bust on his mind. His focus is on a bust of Benjamin Franklin Keith.

Not to slight the late Miss Mansfield, but we're talking about a really big bust here. We're talking about a 500-pound, larger-than-life-sized bust, a stately bronze image of Keith, the New Hampshire native whose impact on show business will forever eclipse that of any contemporary motion picture star.

A bold claim?

It might seem so, especially when you consider that Keith was born and raised in the humble little hamlet of Hillsborough. Lord knows, that's as good a place as any to embark upon a voyage to absolute anonymity, but lo and behold, upon his death in 1914, the venerable *New York Times* recognized him as the man who "founded and began the continuous performance medium now known as vaudeville."

Now, that fact alone might make Mr. Keith a marginally interesting footnote for those of us who are New Hampshire history buffs. The fact that he also came to own the Manchester Opera House further piqued my own interest.

However, after I came across some of the other actors who factor into this show biz saga—American icons like P.T. Barnum, William Randolph Hearst, Thomas Edison and Joseph P. Kennedy—well, then I knew I had the madcap makings for a little Monday morning mayhem.

Where to begin? Certainly not at the beginning.

That was even too boring for young Benjamin, who left Hillsborough in 1853 at the age of seven. After 11 more years of farm life in Massachusetts, he was ready for a spicier slice of life, so he talked his way into a series of odd jobs—purser on a steamship, candy maker and carnival tout for the legendary P.T. Barnum.

Eventually, his travels brought him back to Boston, where, penniless, he took up residence on a bench in Boston Common. That subject never came up in his letters back to the folks on the farm, mostly because the letters were too crammed with his visionary schemes for fame and fortune. All he needed, of course, was the fortune.

Luckily, Benjamin had the good fortune to have a wealthy uncle named Lyman Gerould, who was making a name for himself with a fledgling outfit called the Manchester Gas Company.

After reading of his nephew's impassioned but-half-baked scheme about a clean-shaven, dancing monkey in drag named Baby Alice—don't laugh—Uncle Lyman ponied up $300 and, from that day in 1883, the world of entertainment would never be the same.

(Uncle Lyman would never be the same either. He left Manchester and went on to serve as confidential secretary to legendary publisher William Randolph Hearst, but that's another story for another day).

Today's story?

It's about that bust, remember?

We'll get to it eventually.

For the moment, we are focusing on Benjamin Keith's first foray into the world of entertainment. Baby Alice, the aforementioned monkey, became a money magnet for the young entrepreneur. For one thin dime, improper Bostonians flocked to watch the monkey perform in the window of a vacant storefront at 545 Washington St. that later gained fame as the Gaiety Museum.

In time, the dimes added up. Benjamin and a partner turned the storefront into a downstairs zoo and an upstairs theater, where he tinkered with the revolutionary notion of "continuous performance."

See, back in this Victorian era, there were only two kinds of entertainment. There was legitimate theater that symbolized high culture (and high income) and then there was the vulgar, saloon-oriented, honky-tonk entertainment for the great unwashed.

Benjamin Keith decided to lay claim to that unclaimed middle ground known as the middle class.

He did this by running constant entertainment for 12 hours a day. "Come when you please," he advertised in the Boston papers, "and stay as long as you like."

Many of the performers—singers, comics, lecturers and dancers—would repeat their acts in the course of the day, but customers did stay. (Some even endured deliberately tedious acts called "chasers" that were meant to shoo them away).

Business was so good that in 1892, Keith was able to open his own show place fronting on the Boston Common, "a dream pavilion of vaudeville" which he modestly named the B.F. Keith Theatre.

Although famed vaudeville star Fred Allen once described Keith as a "clod hopper who never lost his bumpkin streak," the New Hampshire farm boy spared no expense on the theater that bore his name.

His architect was the same man who designed the Metropolitan Opera House in New York, and when Thomas Edison unveiled his new kinescope moving picture projector, Keith became the first theater operator to run movies on a daily basis.

That combination of instinct and innovation paid off. Before long, a spin-off business called the Keith Vaudeville Booking Office controlled more than 500 theaters around the country.

Keith himself came to own more than his share of those theaters, with sites in London, New York, Philadelphia and, of course, Manchester. Yes, it was a very big deal indeed when "In a Blaze of Electrical Glory," Keith's company took over the Manchester Opera House in 1906.

Breathless accounts in the *Manchester Mirror and American*—"dazzling; too good to be true"—reported the outlandish expenditure of $11,000 (gasp!) for renovations "because it is said of Mr. Keith that he never does things half-way."

And neither did his friends, many of whom realized vast fortunes due to their alliances with him. After Keith died of heart disease in Palm Springs in 1914—his obituary made the front page of *The Times*—his friends (including Edward Albee, adoptive father of the famed playwright) decided to express their gratitude by erecting the Keith Memorial Theatre in Boston.

It was a $5 million palace, so plush and ornate that it was never meant to show a profit. No, it was to stand as a lasting tribute to Benjamin Franklin Keith, and toward that end, another partner—Joseph P. Kennedy—commissioned an artist to create a bust of his fallen friend.

For nearly 40 years, that stately bust, perched on an ornate marble pedestal, looked down upon theater-goers as they ascended the winding staircases of the grand show place. And then it simply disappeared.

It was discovered quite by accident in 1965. Fred McLennan (remember him?) found it in a ladies room closet at what had become the RKO Keith Memorial Theatre.

"The owner, Ben Sack, was in the smelting business," said Fred, who lives in Dedham, Massachusetts, "and with all the armaments that were being made for Vietnam, I was amazed that he hadn't melted the thing down for scrap."

Instead, Sack gave the bust to Fred, who has stored it for nearly 30 years. Although he is a radio engineer by trade, Fred is a show business historian of the highest order, and the saga of Benjamin Franklin Keith has long been his fascination.,

And as for the bust?

"I'd like to see him return home," Fred said. "I don't know if it should be in Hillsborough or in the State House or in a museum somewhere in New Hampshire, but the fact that he became Mr. Show Business from such humble beginnings means a lot."

But how much?

That's the question posed by Jayme Simoes, spokesman for the Franklin Pierce Homestead in Hillsborough.

"When I talked to Mr. McLennan, he said he was looking for something between $10,000 and $20,000 for the bust," he said. "I understand that Mr. Keith was a very important man in the history of show business and we in Hillsborough are proud of all that he achieved, but our focus has to be on the Franklin Pierce Homestead.

"As an under-funded organization," he added, "if we divert our attention to things that are secondary to our mission, we'd be called to task by our members, and rightfully so. But, if someone wants to buy it and place it in the State House or the Museum of New Hampshire History, I'd certainly support that."

Don't hold your breath on that, though.

"Normally, a piece like that goes to a private collector," said Bill Copeley, librarian with the New Hampshire Historical Society. "I'd probably refer Mr. McLennan to the Currier Gallery of Art or the galleries at UNH or Dartmouth College."

I guess we can consider that referral delivered, but for the right price, Fred would prefer to avoid the auction houses and deliver the bust to someone in New Hampshire.

Unfortunately, his plans just may go bust.

(2/1/99)

Her plastic hard hat identified her as a part of the team when volunteers from the Make-A-Wish Foundation assembled a playground for Rose. (Union Leader Photo by John Clayton)

The Wish

It was cold up here in Benton yesterday. Not winter cold. It was November cold. Gray skies. Bare trees, Spitting snow. It's the raw, rainy kind of cold folks expect this time of year in this remote corner of Grafton County.

In a clearing off Route 116, a dozen guys ignored the damp and the chill and busily clambered about the grounds around a small mobile home. They were building a playground.

It's for a girl named Rose.

She's five years old.

And she's dying.

It would be nice to pretend it wasn't so, but a terminal blood disease doesn't buy into denial. And so it was that a group of volunteers came here yesterday in an early morning caravan that snaked up 1-93 from Manchester, up through the Notches, then west toward this tiny hamlet near Woodsville. It's a town that 330 people call home, last time they counted.

"We're glad we're here, but we're sorry we have to be," said Barbara Breed. She's the executive director of the New Hampshire chapter of the Make-A-Wish Foundation. Rose wished for a playground. And her wish is being granted.

Sometimes the wishes are simple—a puppy, a drum set, bunk beds. Others are more complex, like an audience with the Pope or a visit to the White House, but those are just a few of the wishes the group has granted for 116 terminally ill children since the local chapter was chartered in 1987.

"When they're little, Disney World is what they dream of," Breed said, "but when the kids get older, their wishes get more creative."

Take Jared, an 11-year-old Gilford boy who suffers from a form of Muscular Dystrophy. Maybe it can be traced to his own confinement in a wheelchair, but he developed a fascination with speedy, graceful cheetahs. His wish was to see the cats in their natural habitat.

An impossibility? Not with Make-A-Wish.

Volunteer Dena DeLucca pulled more strings than Papa Gepetto. By the time she was done, Jared and his parents were in the South African nation of Namibia watching cheetahs roam the African veldt.

That wish held special significance for these folks, not so much because of its scope or magnitude, but because it was the 100th wish they had granted. They derive just as much satisfaction from the little wishes. Sometimes more when you're dealing with a kid like this one.

"Right now, almost half of our wishes involve trips to Disney World," said chapter president Brian Carpentier. "That's not just here in New Hampshire. That's the case all over the country and we understand that. The people at Disney treat the kids like royalty, but there's something special about a wish like this one."

See, Rose's playground isn't just for her. She wants it for her brother and sister. They're dying too.

The volunteers who came here yesterday knew that. They knew this little girl in the toy hardhat had a last wish and she wanted something she could share, but when you ask them about it, they can't talk about it for long. They pause in mid-sentence. Then they just look away for a while.

Then they go back to work.

What makes Rose's wish so rewarding to these people is that it's real. It's tangible. The Wish Granters can lift and work and sweat. When their labors are through, they have something to show for their efforts. There's a sense of relief—it's a catharsis, if you're looking for a big word—and it means as much to them as the playground does to Rose.

"It's hard on the Wish Granters especially," Breed said. "You try and tell yourself not to get too attached to these children, but their families are so giving and the kids are so strong. You know, we're not supposed to outlive our children but we do and they see it and these big, burly men are left to cope with emotions they never imagined."

The sense of completion they sought yesterday escaped them. The bulldozer bogged down and the weather was a hindrance but Rose had nothing but smiles so they'll come back again to finish the job. For them, tomorrow means a lot.

"It has to," Carpentier said. "You're helping kids who don't have many tomorrows."

(11/2/95)

Francis Gilman knows a lot about New Hampshire's barns, not to mention the colorful characters that sometimes dwell within. (Union Leader Photo by Bob LaPree)

Something There Is That Doesn't Love a Barn . . .

THERE MAY BE SOMETHING that evokes more of New Hampshire's agricultural heritage than a weathered old barn, but if there is, I can't think of it.

Neither can Francis Gilman.

"I still have a lot of softness in my heart for the old ones," he said, "especially the ones that were 'mortised and tenoned.' Those are the traditional barns, the kind they don't put up any more."

Put them up? More and more, they're taking them down.

It's a three-pronged problem that is confronting these old barns, much like an old-fashioned pitchfork. One prong involves apathy. Another, economics. The third, the elements. Together, those problems may spell the end of these simple structures that epitomize both form and function.

To see that form and function, I got Francis to walk me through an old barn. He's been in most every barn in the state—we'll get to his credentials later—and he chose the one at the old Plummer Homestead over in Milton. The place was home to seven generations of Plummers, who lived, farmed, lumbered and prospered on the land before turning it over to the New Hampshire Farm Museum a few years back.

"This one's been fancied up," he said, "and there's no hand-hewn timbers, but it's a good example. The floors are eastern hemlock, as most of them were. Down in southern New England, the beams would be made of chestnut. Connecticut was loaded with chestnut, but here in New Hampshire, the beams were typically pine."

The reason? A century ago, no one building a barn was going to pay to haul in boards. Barns were no-frills things, made of locally available materials. Like pine. If a farmer wanted style, he bought his wife a dress. Barns were about work.

A lot of that work involved hay.

"In the old days," Francis said, gesturing both left and right, "the barns were big enough to drive right through, with big doors on each end. They'd haul the hay wagon into the barn, then pitch the loose hay up onto the first loft. Then they'd climb up onto that loft and pitch it up another level to a loft in the middle. That way they were using up all the space in the barn, right up to the rafters."

While the hay helped insulate the barn, its primary purpose was as feed for the livestock—mostly cows—that lived in the barn. After following a precise biological path through the digestive system of those cows—I think you know what I'm talking about—that same hay continued to provide another kind of insulation.

It's best to turn this delicate narrative over to Francis.

"Most barns had something they called a barn cellar," he explained. "It was right below the stalls where you kept the cows. They built scuttles into the floor—it was like a trap door with handles—and those were called 'manure scuttles.'

"All you had to do was open the scuttles and shove the manure down the chute. Once in a while they'd put the pigs down there just to let them even out the piles. Come spring, the place would be pretty much full, but it was perfect storage for manure, which was a pretty valuable product."

The farmers also knew that manure's value as fertilizer was almost equaled by its value as insulation.

"When they stopped using the barn for animal storage, the foundations of the barns just went to pieces," Francis said. "Part of it was because most of them were built on rock foundations that had just been laid on the ground.

"Without the manure in the cellar for insulation, the frost action started setting in, then the rock foundations started heaving and the barns would start twisting and falling. They needed the insulation from the manure."

Truth be told, the old-fashioned barns don't have much practical use today and when they stand idle—as most of them do—decay is inevitable.

Francis doesn't like to admit that, but it's a fact. He should know. He's 72, and he's been around dairy farms since he was born. Before his retirement, he spent 20 years as an agricultural engineer with the UNH Cooperative Extension Service helping farmers keep up with the times.

"Most old farmers resist change," he smiled.

So do barns.

"They don't adapt well," he said. "In the age when they were built, they were perfect, but if you try and run plumbing in there, the pipes will freeze in winter. That means you have to close them up and insulate them, but if you keep livestock in them, it gets too damp. You get so much moisture, it can get so it's like it's raining inside."

In short, old barns have become anachronisms, products of another day. In their day, however, they helped farm families survive. Francis knows. Without a barn, you couldn't keep the cows that kept milk on the table. That milk meant cream and cheese and butter. And how important was butter? Francis explains it best through his father's eyes.

"My father used to tell how one time he was over at the neighbors' farm eating an evening meal—of course, that was supper—and he got to dippin' pretty heavy in the butter," Francis explained, only the word "supper" sounded like "suppah" and "butter" sounded more like "buttah."

"Well after watchin' him for a while, the woman, she said 'Just a minute young man and I'll assist you to the fat,' but the fat was probably something left over from the salt pork they'd fried, which didn't taste nearly so good as the butter.

"Thing is, they needed the butter for money. They'd sell it for salt and spices and sugar and things they couldn't produce themselves."

Those days of family farms are almost gone, of course, and if we're not careful, the barns will soon be gone too.

"There are a lot of issues to address," said Nancy Dutton, director of the state's Division of Historic Resources. "One involves taxes. People who buy the farms with these barns are being taxed for them. If they fix them up, they're afraid their taxes will go up. If they can't afford the taxes, they tear them down."

One group, the Land and Community Heritage Commission, is exploring the issue. Its members are looking into long-term conservation funding for cultural and historic resources, and barns fall into that category.

"They're landmarks," Nancy said. "We promote agricultural properties as part of the New Hampshire experience, and the variety of barns we have in the state reflect not only the different times of construction, but different ethnic heritages, too.

"And it's not just barns," she added. "We're losing out-buildings like silos and poultry sheds and corn cribs, sugar houses, smoke houses, all things that were once part of the landscape."

That landscape is changing. Barns are falling. And when the last one is gone, a little bit of who we are will go with it.

(10/21/98)

Celtic Savior

ACCORDING TO THOSE who were there, patrons who saw Tony Lavelli perform at Boston Garden for the first time on Dec. 22, 1949, all walked out muttering the same thing: "That kid can play."

But what kid were they talking about?

Were they talking about the rangy 6-foot-4 kid who totally outplayed George Mikan—simply the best basketball player in the known world at that time—to lead the Boston Celtics to an 87-69 victory over the world champion Minneapolis Lakers?

Or were they talking about the virtuoso kid—the gangly musical prodigy—who came out in his warm-ups at halftime and bedazzled the crowd of 5,206 with his accordion rendition of "Lady of Spain"?

Doesn't matter.

They were all talking about the same Tony Lavelli.

There are times when I think the expression "renaissance man" is overused. Not in the case of Tony Lavelli, however. The man was many, many things—All-American athlete, Ivy League scholar, accomplished performer and composer—and until last week, when he died at the age of 71, he was one other thing—a quiet, unassuming resident of Laconia, New Hampshire.

That's where I met him about 10 years ago, in the modest home he kept on Union Avenue. It was a close, cluttered warren filled with newspapers and photographs, posters and sheet music. It was to be the launching pad for his competitive assault on the "Star Spangled Banner."

That's how he got me up there. After composing as many as 5,000 songs, he had penned a number called "Take Pride in the USA," and he was convinced it would one day become our National Anthem. I

Whether he was working with a basketball or an accordion, the late Tony Lavelli always delivered a stellar performance for the Boston Celtics. (Photo Courtesy of Doris Lavelli Duff)

took the bait, but it was only after I found out about his "other" life that I was hooked on his story.

The song? That was going nowhere, but as I soon discovered, it was clear from an early age that Tony Lavelli was going places.

The first place was Yale.

After winning athletic and academic acclaim at Somerville (Mass.) High School, he headed to New Haven in 1945 to study music. Because World War II had depleted the ranks of college athletics, freshmen won the rare chance to compete at the varsity level, and Tony took advantage by winning All-American honors right out of the gate.

Before his college career was over, he was the subject of a time-lapse photo spread in *Life* magazine that labeled his hook shot "the most spectacular offensive weapon in college basketball history." By the time he was through, he was a four-time All-American and the highest scorer in college basketball history with 1,964 points.

More important to him, however, was his music degree and being immersed in life on one of America's most fascinating college campuses.

"When we were at Yale, we had the secret society known as the 'Skull and Bones,'" Tony said, "and in 1948, the number one 'tap' of that organization was a very popular All-American baseball player named George Bush.

"One day near the end of his senior year, he came up to me in the courtyard and tapped me on the shoulder, which made me the number one 'tap' for my year. It was a great honor, and when I signed with the Celtics, he wrote me a nice letter from Houston where he was starting up his oil business, just to congratulate me."

A year later, when it was Tony's turn to "tap," he broke the All-American string by designating a less-athletic successor to lead the "Skull and Bones Society." Instead of a jock, he chose a promising but little known writer and speaker. Some guy named William F. Buckley Jr.

The "Skull and Bones" may be a secret society, but there was nothing secret about Tony's achievements. Certainly, they didn't escape the notice of the wily Walter Brown, owner of the struggling Boston franchise in what was then the fledgling National Basketball Association. He needed a gate attraction to bring in fickle fans, and Tony—a homegrown hero with talent, looks and a unique marketing spin—filled the bill as his first round draft choice.

"The deal was that I would play basketball for the Celtics for $13,000," Tony explained, "and be guaranteed half-time accordion performances for 25 NBA games at $125 each."

If Brown was thrilled with the results, Tony was indifferent.

"I always said basketball was my hobby," he said, "but show business was my life." That was to be expected from a guy who made his radio debut on NBC at age 13 and his stage debut at New York's Roxy Theater alongside Donald O'Connor at 19.

Thus, after one season, Tony left the Celtics for the ultimate marriage of sports and entertainment—the Harlem Globetrotters. The team lived up to its name in the three years Tony was on board. He captained the opposition "all-stars," played his accordion in gyms and music halls all over the world and he even co-wrote songs with Globetrotters owner Abe Saperstein, but even that grew tiresome.

So he left.

Walked away.

It was unthinkable. The man viewed by many as the most talented player in the game simply up and left to pursue something he loved. Why, it would be like Michael Jordan leaving basketball to play baseball.

Okay, bad example, but, at the height of his prowess and earning power, Tony left basketball to pursue a career in entertainment, and you know what?

He never looked back.

At the start, his notoriety and the novelty of his act won him bookings in New York, Miami and Los Angeles with the likes of Ed Sullivan, Jackie Gleason and Arthur Godfrey. Later, the bookings got smaller, and so did the towns. Butte, Kenosha, Fort Wayne. But even in his 60s, when his bookings had dropped off and his songs weren't selling and retirement had brought him to Laconia, he still knew that, in his heart, he made the right choice.

"I just remind myself that Van Gogh sold only one painting in his lifetime," he said, "and then his painting 'Sunflowers' went for millions."

In the end—Tony's came at the age of 71—he never made a sale like that. He never came close, but he was still one in a million.

(1/14/98)

The Gold Rush

YOU WOULDN'T KNOW IT to look at, say, Deion Sanders, but scientists claim that 98 percent of the gold on the earth is still *in* the earth. It's that simple fact that gives Jeff Orchard reason to get out of bed in the morning.

He's a prospector.

Not the weenie kind. He's not one of those guys who wears black socks and wing tips while prowling the beach with a mine-sweeper in a life-and-death search for pocket change. He's a gold prospector.

He's also a former firefighter, windmill builder and glider pilot who makes his living as an environmental wetland scientist, but in his free time, he's a prospector. By his own admission, it's an avocation that raises more eyebrows than it does money.

"Some people are mystified as to why I'll spend $30 for gas, drive for hours and go without lunch so I can shovel dirt standing thigh-deep in cold water for six or eight hours," he shrugged. "I keep telling them it's better for me than television."

Now that we're heavily into reruns, there's no refuting his logic. As such, he regularly leaves his Windham home and scours the brooks and streams and river beds of New Hampshire in search of gold, gobs of which may be there for the taking.

The only catch?

You have to find it first.

Personally, I think it would be far more convenient if they just stored the gold in clearly marked bins on the side of the road, but then I never would have had the chance to meet Willie Ford.

You've heard of the "Old Man of the Mountain?" Jeff refers to Willie as the "Gold Man of the Mountain." He makes his home over in Charlestown now, but if you asked him, he'd probably tell you

Scouring the pan for signs of gold are prospectors Jeff Orchard, left, and Willie Ford during an outing on the Amonoosuc River. (Union Leader Photo by John Clayton)

he's just as much at home in the middle of the Wild Ammonoosuc River in Bath, which is where he was Tuesday.

"Anybody who thinks they're gonna make a livin' at this ain't gonna eat very good," said Willie, who, at 72, isn't about to squander any of his gold in gilding the lily. "It's a hobby, just like huntin' and fishin.'"

Funny. Even as he spoke, he was doing both. Huntin' behind large rocks for likely deposit points and fishin' out pans of gravel.

"The best place to look for gold is where fast moving water loses its velocity quickly," Jeff explained. "Generally, that's behind boulders and on the inside of a bend in the river."

The reason? The churning water carries particles of gold downstream along with the rest of the sediment. Since gold is far heavier than the other materials—it's also 19 times heavier than water—it settles faster when the water goes slower.

A bunch of other stuff settles too—like magnetite, gamet and buckshot—and watching Willie separate those elements with a gentle swirling motion of his miner's pan is akin to watching a French chef fret over an omelette.

Of course, that simple pan is like a quaint ancestral artifact of prospecting. There are a lot more sophisticated tools of the trade—a motorized dredge, for one—but on this day, Willie and Jeff seemed perfectly content with a small sluice, their pans and shovels.

"In fact, there's an old saying that the only sure way to make money in a gold rush is to sell shovels," laughed Jeff, who included that adage in a book he's written on the subject of prospecting hereabouts.

He called it *Gold in New Hampshire*. I think it should have been *Gold? In New Hampshire?* because people are often shocked to hear those words in the same sentence. Maybe it's because "gold" is such a visceral word. It's a word that provokes a gut reaction. Like "shark." Or "taxes."

"But it's here," said Jeff, whose book lists gold finds in towns like Lebanon and Plainfield and the one at the Dodge Mine up in Lyman back in 1870. "It produced $46,000 worth of gold. Back then, gold was valued at $10 an ounce. In today's market? You figure it out."

I did. Considering that gold closed in New York yesterday at $390.30 an ounce, if you happened to stumble upon that Lyman mother lode today, it would bring home a cool $1.8 million.

To be honest, I fell a little bit short of that in my prospecting debut. For an hour's work, I got a flake of gold about the size of this capital "0." I've seen larger flakes of dandruff, but before you begin to think that Willie and Jeff are flakes, let me disabuse you of that notion. They're strong advocates for a kind of prospecting etiquette that is equal parts law and common sense.

For example, you don't need a license to use a shovel and a miner's pan, but if you're going to use a motorized dredge, you need a permit from the State of New Hampshire. It costs $25. If you're going on private property, you also need permission of the landowner. Failure to do so costs more than money. It can lead to lost opportunity.

"I haven't met a recreational miner yet who didn't have a high regard for the environment," Jeff said, "but I also know there are some inconsiderate fools out there. If we just use a little common sense and have some respect for the property rights of others, we'll be welcomed back."

In a way, Jeff has become the Emily Post of miners. His book spells out the protocol of prospecting and it's also something of a clearinghouse for equipment shops, magazines and information on clubs like the Northeast Recreational Gold Miners Association.

Here in New Hampshire, it's the book by which all others on the topic will be judged. I guess that makes it the gold standard.

(4/27/96)

Take a Seat

STILL TRYING TO FIGURE OUT which party won the most seats in the last election? Stop counting. Nobody has more seats than Alphonse Plourde.

The garage at his home in Gilmanton is full of them. It's a veritable sea of seats, rugged cast iron contraptions that once propped up farmers on their plows and harrows and reapers and mowers and cultivators and harvesters and other assorted implements of agriculture.

Today, those seats are viewed as a form of agrarian folk art, and with 300 seats to his name, Al claims he has the biggest collection in New Hampshire.

And what's the best seat in the house?

"This one," he said, hefting a rugged green number. "It's called 'The Star of Vermont.' It's worth a thousand, maybe fifteen hundred dollars."

Al isn't flying by the seat of his pants when he makes such a claim, either. He's a member of the Cast Iron Seat Collector Association, a national organization that has cataloged more than 2,200 types of iron seats. Each is rated by quality and availability. Naturally, the rarer the seat, the higher the price.

These seats began appearing as early as 1850, but the majority of them were manufactured after the Civil War, when munitions factories were converted to civilian use. By 1900, production slowed, then stopped. Then the collecting started.

An odd hobby? Perhaps, but people will collect anything. You name it, people collect it, from buttons to beer cans to Bugattis. Mickey Rooney collected wives. Maynard G. Krebs collected tinfoil. My own personal friend Paul Regner collected baseball caps. He had 1,500.

Even though he can only sit on one at a time, Alphonse Plourde of Gilmanton is the state's leading collector of antique cast iron seats. (Union Leader Photo by Bob LaPree)

Fifteen hundred hats. One head. Go figure.

Anyway, historians figure that putting cast iron seats on farm implements was a major step for agriculture because it saved steps for farmers. The seats enabled them to ride instead of walking behind their machines.

Still, you have to wonder. Why cast iron?

I mean, given the cold weather that New Hampshire farmers encountered in the early spring and late fall, and given the specific portion of the anatomy that came into contact with the seat—Yow!—why cast iron?

"I don't know about that," Al said, "but when they stopped making cast iron, they went to pressed tin, and tin seats ain't worth anything to a collector."

He should know. His collection includes seats from all over the United States—it extends, you might say, from seat to shining seat—as well as Canada, England, even New Zealand. He prefers the domestic product, however, and his prized New Hampshire find is called the "Granite No. 2." He showed it to me.

"In 1860, they were making mowing machines at a foundry over in Lebanon," he grunted, "but the things got so heavy, the horses couldn't draw it."

And Al could hardly lift it. It's not because he's 75. He's a retired mason with hands like vise grips. It's because the seat is dead weight, and he's smart enough to wear steel-toed boots when he picks it up.

He's picked up a lot of things over the years. He used to collect and refinish old steamer trunks—he sold maybe a hundred, he said—and now he's into vintage high chairs. He has about 30 around his house, which looks out on Rocky Pond.

"And then I have my egg beaters," he said.

Hen fruit wouldn't stand a chance in this place. Hand-operated egg beaters of every size and shape hang from the rafters like stalactites. He has more than 400 of them, an odd counterpoint to his expanding collection of 20 ceramic chickens.

"I sold an egg beater for $600 last week," he said, "but I don't want to sell off any more singles. If someone wants the whole collection, that's fine, but I'm not in this to make money. I'm in it to make friends."

He finds those friends at auctions, yard sales and antique shops, where owners maintain a constant vigil for his favorite items.

They're getting harder to find though—the cast iron seats in particular—which means he has to go farther afield to feed his habit.

"Every day, I go out looking," he said. "One day I'm in Vermont, next day I'm in Epsom, next day I might drive up to Canada. I could fly out to all the big auctions," he added, "but how am I going to get them home on the plane?"

Well, he could always buy a seat for the seats.

But that's not Al's style.

His wife, Priscilla, pointed that out while I was reminding Al that there's a fine line between a hobby and mental illness. She laughed.

"We drove all the way to New Brunswick one day," Priscilla said, cringing at the recollection of the 10-hour drive. "We were there for 10 minutes and he didn't find anything good, so I asked if we were going to stay over and he said, 'No. We'll drive home. With the money we save, we can buy another seat.'"

Three hundred seats. One butt. Go figure.

(11/5/98)

The Burger King

HE'S NOT THE KIND OF GUY to bite the hand that has fed him—the same hand that has fed 90 billion others in the 14,000 restaurants that bear his name—but then again, Richard McDonald isn't the kind of guy to pull his punches either, even when you ask him how he feels about hamburgers.

"I prefer hot dogs," he says.

Wow. Tell me George Steinbrenner roots for the Red Sox. Lee Iacocca drives a Toyota. Heck, tell me Jack Daniels drinks milk. I'll believe anything now.

Given his druthers, Richard McDonald, co-founder of the burger joint that spawned the most phenomenally successful restaurant chain on this or any other planet would prefer a hot dog—grilled, with mustard—thank you very much.

Hey, somebody fire up the hibachi! It's the least we can do for the man who is living proof that the American dream is alive and well and living in Manchester.

Okay, okay. You got me. Dick McDonald lives in Bedford these days, but don't think for a minute that he's gone uptown on us.

This is a man whose rags-to-riches saga would make Horatio Alger blush, yet he is as modest and unassuming as the guy behind you in the checkout line at Sully's Superette. In fact, he probably is the guy behind you at Sully's.

He still shops there, just a couple of blocks from his parents' old house at 500 South Main St., the one across the street from the firehouse where Captain Arnold let him ring the bell on Armistice Day, November 11, 1918, the day World War I ended.

"I was eight years old, and climbing up on that truck and ringing that bell was the biggest thrill of my life," McDonald said.

Must have been some thrill, because this is a life where the list of

His rags-to-riches saga would make Horatio Alger blush, but for Richard McDonald, success was always about coming home to New Hampshire. (Photo Courtesy of Gale French)

thrills includes accepting a check for $2.7 million from an egomaniacal crank named Ray Kroc, but I'm getting ahead of myself here.

Let's begin by saying that the McDonald clan lived under modest circumstances during Dick's childhood, what with his father, Patrick McDonald, supporting a wife and five kids on his salary from the G.P. Krafts Shoe Co.

Since such modest circumstances precluded college, Dick took his diploma from West High School in 1927 and headed west, partly to dodge the economic bullet of The Great Depression but mostly to join his brother, Maurice.

"We had an uncle who was a detective in Hollywood, and he got my brother a job at Columbia Pictures, so I went too," McDonald said. "We pushed lights, we drove trucks, we even got to see stars like Clara Bow and the Barrymores. For a kid from New Hampshire, making 25 bucks a week, it was like Heaven."

When Heaven got to look like a professional dead end, the McDonald brothers took over a movie theater in Glendora. Next they tried their hand at a hot dog stand near the Santa Anita Raceway, and then, in 1940, (if this were a movie, the music would be getting louder now) they opened a drive-in restaurant in San Bernardino, a happenin' little town that history will remember as the home of the Hell's Angels, the Seventh Day Adventists and the original McDonald's Drive-In Restaurant.

By 1948 the place was quite a success, but it was only a buy-a-Cadillac, live-in-a-mansion, ho-hum success. That wasn't quite enough for the McDonald brothers. Thus, Dick and his brother—everyone knew Maurice as Mac—began to tinker with their concept.

"For instance, we had a huge barbecue pit with wood chips shipped in from Arkansas, but when we went back over three years of receipts, we found that 80 percent of our business was hamburgers," he said. "The more we pushed the barbecue, the more hamburgers we sold."

Their decision? In restaurant lingo? Eighty-six the barbecue.

But they didn't stop there. They cleaned house. They eighty-sixed their car hops, they eighty-sixed their dishwashers, they even eighty-sixed the dishes.

For three months, the McDonald brothers shuttered their shop, and when they reopened their doors, well . . . they didn't have any doors. They had windows. Self-service windows, and the windows were the only things that needed washing, because they also had paper bags and paper cups.

What they had done amounted to addition by subtraction. By eliminating the car hop—the drive-in equivalent of the middleman—they had taken the food service industry and distilled it to its very essence. Now they were getting the food directly to the customer, in the shortest time possible—special orders do upset us—and at the lowest possible price, because Dick and Mac had decided to hang their hats on volume.

"Everyone else was getting 35 cents for a burger? Fine, we sold them for 15 cents," Dick recalled. "Cheeseburgers were 19 cents. Fries were a dime. So was a Coke. Our most expensive item was 20 cents. That was a shake."

And it was the shake that shook the restaurant world to its very core. By 1954, the McDonald boys were already on the cover of *American Restaurant Magazine* (you mean you don't read it?) when a shake machine salesman (the aforementioned Kroc) stopped by to see why one restaurant needed eight of his machines to keep up with demand.

The rest, as they say, is history. Kroc was hired on as a franchising agent, and by 1961, the brothers sold it to him for their price—a million apiece plus seven hundred grand for taxes—and retired in permanent comfort.

While his brother passed away in 1971, Dick—at age 84—continues to live the life he envisioned (alongside his high school sweetheart, the former Dorothy Jones) before he revolutionized the dining industry.

It was Dick McDonald who streamlined food production, it was Dick McDonald who pioneered self-service and it was Dick McDonald who gave the world the Golden Arches, which first went up locally in Manchester on May 5, 1964.

Without Dick McDonald, there'd be no McNuggets, no McMuffins, no McNothing, and they know it when he stops in at the Second Street McDonald's for lunch. Imagine the pressure? It's like singing for Frank Sinatra. Telling jokes to Bob Hope. Showing your navel to Madonna.

"Yeah, I guess it's like pitching to Babe Ruth," said owner Ron Evans.

There's just one thing that bothers me. It's this "Burger King" thing. Don't get me wrong. Great company, good food, clean restaurants, "hold the pickle, hold the lettuce" and all that stuff, but I have a problem with the name.

There's only one burger king. His name is Dick McDonald. Manchester's own. The undisputed heavyweight champion of burgerdom. The Father of Fast Food. *Ein Burger Meister*. King Richard the First. The Burger King.

To which I can only say, long live The King.

(6/14/93)

Spanning the Ages

THINK YOUR DAY AT THE OFFICE is filled with ups and downs?

You should be Barry White.

One minute his desk might be 20 feet above the mouth of the Piscataqua River in Portsmouth. Next thing you know, he's 170 feet above the churning waters that, depending upon the tides, flow in and out of the Atlantic Ocean.

Barry's the senior operator on the fabled Memorial Bridge, an engineering marvel—the bridge, not Barry—that will celebrate its 75th birthday next week.

I'd like to tell you the storied deck-span draw bridge is unique, but it's not. Still, it was only the third of its kind built in America—its predecessors were in Portland, Oregon, and Jacksonville, Florida—and its quirky appeal is undeniable.

Is it functional? Certainly.

Just as countless boats make their way under the bridge every day, countless cars make their way across this still-vital link between Maine and New Hampshire. As bridges go, though, the Memorial Bridge is just as much about style as substance.

That was obvious from the outset.

For instance, when the niceties of the dedication ceremonies were completed on Aug. 17, 1923, *The Manchester Union* reported that "pandemonium broke forth and an avalanche of traffic rushed in both directions."

Further evidence of public passion? "Two miles of automobiles dashed across the bridge," *The Union* reported, "and many boys raced on foot and bicycles to see who would be the first to reach the opposite shore."

Even today, bicyclists and joggers are staples on the span,

He's been working on the Memorial Bridge for years, but Don Stevens still gets a rise out of his vertical voyages above the Piscataqua River in Portsmouth. (Union Leader Photo by John Clayton)

which—given its predictably punctual vertical voyages—makes it a great spot for conversation.

"I think that's why Joe Moulton still likes to work on the bridge," said Don Stevens, construction superintendent with the state's bureau of bridge management. "He's retired, but when he works as a gatekeeper, he's like our goodwill ambassador. When the bridge is up, he likes to be out on the sidewalk so he can talk to all the ladies. It makes the whole thing a little more personal."

True. It's hard to get steamed about a bridge-related, traffic tie-up when a guy like Joe starts explaining how the bridge works. And, in the interest of gender equity, you should know that, after 75 years, the bridge is now the workplace of Linda Newman, its first full-time female gatekeeper.

In an age of automation, it's nice to see human beings still come out and lower the gate when the siren sounds. Generally, as a concession to mariners, that sound comes every half hour from May 15 through Oct. 31.

"There are exceptions," Don said. "Like if we have a big ship coming in, anything over 100 tons, we open on demand. Same goes for the Coast Guard. They can get us to open any time they need it. Otherwise, it's every half hour if needed and after Oct. 31, it's on demand."

And demand for the bridge itself reached a fever pitch in the days following what we now know as World War I. The reason? Access to the Portsmouth Naval Shipyard on the Kittery side of the Piscataqua.

"It's hard to visualize now, but the men would come down with their lunch boxes and ferry across the river and at the end of the day, they'd take the ferry back. It would leave from what was the coal wharf at Prescott Park," said former Portsmouth Mayor Eileen Foley.

"I don't know what we ever would have done in World War II if the men had to use a ferry to get to the shipyard," added Foley, whose knowledge of the fabled bridge goes well beyond its political and economic significance.

Back in 1923, when all of the assorted dignitaries had gathered on the span for its grand opening, the scene was stolen by an adorable five-year-old girl named Eileen Dondero—now Eileen Foley—who was chosen to cut the ribbon. Why her?

"I really don't know," she laughed. "A lady just called up the night before and said 'We'd like one of the Dondero girls to cut the ribbon.' One of my sisters had just lost a tooth, and since one was older and one was younger, I guess they just picked me."

Who knew that 75 years later, that little girl would remain the equivalent of Port City royalty, one whose recollections are as vivid as they were that day.

"I had this lovely orange *crepe de Chine* dress, and they brought me from the park over to the bridge," she said. "The governor of Maine (Percival R. Baxter) and the governor of New Hampshire (Albert 0. Brown) were both there, and I remember the whole day was just marvelous."

Three months later, on Armistice Day, plaques were unveiled on both sides of the bridge. Travelers heading north from Portsmouth are greeted by the following legend: "Memorial to the Sailors and Soldiers Of New Hampshire Who Participated in the World War 1917-1919."

At that time, the bridge symbolized a remarkable collaboration amongst the states of Maine and New Hampshire and the federal government. The $2 million price tag was split amongst the three parties—"Can you imagine what it would cost today?" asked Foley—and continuing maintenance costs also are shared.

The partnership is almost as smooth as the vertical ride.

"You could be standing on the deck and you'd be 10 feet in the air before you even know you're moving," Don Stevens explained. "It takes about three minutes to go all the way up to 150 feet for a full open. Maybe it's because it's all electric, but you can hardly tell you're moving."

Pretty efficient for a 300-foot span that weighs 800 tons. Equally efficient is the rapport between boaters and bridge operators.

"Say we get a sailboat that calls for a 40-foot height," said bridge operator Glen Pike. "We take the bridge up 40 feet so actually, it's a 60-foot lift because even at high tide, we have at least 20 feet to play with from the bridge deck to the water. We use that 20 feet for a safety measure.

"After a while, you get so you can look down and tell," he said. "A guy might radio and ask for 40 feet and you can see he has a 75-foot mast. Sometimes they give you the length of the boat and not the height of the mast, so you learn to watch."

And people still gather to watch the bridge in action. They gaze in amazement, young and old, from the decks at local restaurants and from the decks of the tourist boats that pass beneath the span.

For most of them, it's a bridge that spans a river.

For people like Eileen Foley, it's a bridge that spans the ages.

(8/12/98)

The Last Boy in Blue

GIVEN THE ANNUAL HOOPLA surrounding Independence Day, you can understand why the anniversary of the Battle of Gettysburg—which ran from July 1–3 in 1863—might go unnoticed by all but a handful of Civil War scholars.

And maybe, just maybe, by those who remember James Marion Lurvey.

Lurvey was the last survivor of Gettysburg. He was there as a drummer boy attached to the Union Army of the Potomac and when he died in 1950 at the age of 102, he had outlived every one of New Hampshire's 33,937 Civil War veterans. He's buried in Londonderry, just down the road from the home in the Manchester area of Goffe's Falls where he spent the last 60 years of his life.

The most important year of that life, however, was 1863.

The events of that year—more specifically, James Lurvey's role in those events—have consumed Jay S. Hoar, a professor of English at the University of Maine at Farmington. He has invested 40 years of research into the Civil War service of New Hampshire's "Last Boy in Blue."

"It's ruled my life," Hoar said of Lurvey's story. "I was 16 years old when I met him. It was 1949. I'd never been away from home, but when I saw his picture in *Life* magazine, I knew I had to meet him."

Hoar hitched a ride from his Maine home to Plymouth, New Hampshire, then hopped a train to Manchester. After a night in the Floyd Hotel—"It was three dollars a night," he said—he took a city bus to Lurvey's home at 2915 Brown Ave.

Hoar's visit is a story unto itself, but the story Lurvey told Hoar qualifies as pure Americana.

James Lurvey was just 14 years old when he enlisted in the Union Army. His mother allowed it simply because he was going to serve

James Marion Lurvey was the last survivor of the Battle of Gettysburg, but there was another battle—one with the law—still awaiting the Union Army drummer boy. (Photo Courtesy of Cora Lurvey Smith and Professor Jay S. Hoar)

with his father, Lt. James T. Lurvey, then 36, who was commander of Company A of the 40th Massachusetts.

"I remember Grampa once told me that when people asked why he wanted to join the fighting, he said 'For the Negroes,'" his granddaughter recalled. "Then he went on to explain that he had never seen a Negro."

The frail boy hadn't seen much at all, really. Certainly nothing that could prepare him for the horrors he was to witness.

Hoar's research found both father and son at Dumfries, Virginia, in December of 1862, when Confederate Gen. J.E.B. Stuart tried to disrupt Union supply lines. While his father went on to further battle at the Siege of Suffolk in April and May of 1863, young James—weak and sickly—went on to Campbell Hospital in Washington.

"It was mainly so he could gain strength and return to duty," Hoar said.

When young James was released from the so-called "Invalid Corps," he was ordered north to Pennsylvania, where, in Hoar's words, "the Confederate invasion promised an impending battle of unknown magnitude."

At Gettysburg, that battle was joined on July 1. Young James did not arrive until the next day.

"But July 3 and very probably July 4—could he have eliminated any two days of the 37,554 that he lived—surely they would have been these," Hoar said.

Lurvey's recollections:

"I never fired a shot," he said. "At Gettysburg, I was still a drummer boy (but) during much of that battle I served in the Medical Corps. Shot and shell and the screams of dying men and boys filled the humid air. A non-com told me to put away my drum. He tied a red rag around my left arm and told me I was now in the Medical Corps.

"I told him I was not big enough to lift my end of a stretcher, so he assigned me to a field tent," Lurvey added. "It was stifling inside. I thought I'd keel over when they told me my assignment. Wish then I could have hefted a stretcher.

"I was to stand by and carry out the soldiers' arms and legs as the doctor amputated them," he said. "I guess that was the day I grew up and left boyhood forever. And I wasn't yet sixteen."

His daughter, Cora (Lurvey) Smith, died in Londonderry 10 years ago at the age of 100, but she, too, was fascinated by her father's stories of Gettysburg.

"I recall his saying that one hot day, he crawled into a pup tent in the shade and went to sleep. Soon after, someone pulled him out by the feet and told him a soldier had just died of smallpox in that tent. Luckily, he didn't contract it.

"He said many times when crossing a river or pond, some big strong soldier would take him across on his back," she said. "Many times water to drink was scarce, and after a rain, the men were glad to drink from pools made by cavalry hoofs."

It's hard to gauge the after-effects of such psychological trauma on a boy, but three months later, young James was discharged at Portsmouth. The documents state: "By reason of youth—age 15—not robust."

"During the next 10 months," Hoar said, "he recuperated, added stature and strength and decided to try and improve on what he may have felt was an unimpressive military record."

To do so, he re-enlisted. It was during this second tour of duty, while at Monson Hill Camp near Falls Church, Virginia, that he first set eyes on the man whose integrity had called him to duty.

"He used to visit us in camp," young James said of President Abraham Lincoln. "He was no great sight—tall and awkward—but he had a great mind. He used to talk with us for the sake of cheering us up, I think."

Two months after Robert E. Lee's surrender at Appomattox, Lurvey was discharged from the Union Army. After working in the mica mines and traveling the world on a merchant marine clipper ship, he fell in love with school teacher Sarah McConnell of Haverhill, N.H. They married in 1874.

Raising four daughters in Goffe's Falls should have provided his remaining years with all the excitement he needed, but the legend of James M. Lurvey was not yet complete. In 1902, that legend took on even more mythical proportions when, at the age of 55, he was accused of robbing an American Express payroll—Butch Cassidy-like—from the Goffe's Falls train station that was bound for the local Devonshire Mill.

Although he constantly proclaimed his innocence, he was convicted. The jury asked for leniency—citing his war record—but he was sentenced to serve six to ten years in prison. When he was released, he seemed none the worse for the wear. He even managed to attend the 50th anniversary gathering at Gettysburg in 1913.

To this day, neighborhood children like Esther (Dancause) Theodore remember him well.

"We all knew who he was, that he had been in the Civil War," she said. "I can still remember walking to school in the morning. He'd be sitting on the porch and he'd always wave to us."

He did that until well past his one hundredth birthday. He told friends one of his proudest possessions was the congratulatory letter he had received from President Harry S Truman on that special occasion.

And as to the cause of his longevity? Well, Lurvey always attributed that to his sturdy ancestors and his "fortified" breakfast, a daily dose of coffee spiked with a shot of brandy he called his morning "oh be joyful."

That formula worked until June of 1949. That's when, two months after his wife passed away his daughter, Gladys Lurvey, reluctantly moved him into the Bedford (Mass.) Veterans Hospital.

"Gettysburg was tough," he told Hoar, "but old age is even worse. I'm older now than I ever wished to be. Nobody realizes old age is a hard life till they get there."

That hard life ended on Sept. 17, 1950, but thanks to Hoar, the legend of New Hampshire's "Last Boy in Blue" still lives on.

(7/3/98)

You have to tip your cap to the members of the Conner clan, who have been bottling and capping their own line of Squamscot Beverages since 1863. (Union Leader Photo by John Clayton)

A Tonic for the Soul

YES, I KNOW WE LIVE in New Hampshire and I know that change comes slow in these parts, but if you want to get a handle on how much things *have* changed, just go into a convenience store, walk up to the teenager at the cash register and ask where they keep the "tonic."

Maybe in Gonic they still call it tonic.

Everywhere else, it's soda.

These days, a tonic is something that restores your good spirits. Come to think of it, a visit to Squamscot Beverages in Newfields—where they still make soda pop the way they did 135 years ago—is just that, a tonic for the soul.

Of course, not everything's the same.

Their trademark, seven-ounce, returnable bottles are being phased out. The painted labels on the bottles have been replaced by paper and the cartons—once made of rugged hardwood—are made of cardboard these days.

Yes, change is slowly creeping up on the folks at Conner Bottling Works, but the one constant, the one thing that keeps customers calling for Squamscot Beverages is what you get when you pop the top.

"It doesn't get any fresher than this," said 20-year-old Dan Conner as he handed me a bottle of lemon-lime right off the bottling line. He took one too. His was gone in a flash of neon green. It was one of a dozen sodas that Dan will down on this day, a day like any other for the young man who represents the fifth generation of Conners in the bottling business.

It was 1863 when Dan's great-great-grandfather, William H. Conner, started up a bottling business in Portsmouth. It would be misleading for me to imply that soft drinks were his primary product back then, because—as an old newspaper story in the family archives puts it—"the tonic business . . . was always subservient to the sale of harder drinks."

Translation? William Conner bottled beer, and when he moved his operation from Portsmouth to Newfields, the folks at the Eldridge Brewing Co. simply loaded the beer in hogsheads and hauled it 10 miles west by horse and wagon so he could bottle it for local consumption.

As a sideline, the eldest Conner made an old-fashioned non-alcoholic drink called spruce beer. By the time Prohibition arrived—and regular beer became taboo—Alfred Conner Sr. shifted his father's operation exclusively into soft drinks.

In time, he passed the business onto a third generation, his son, Alfred Jr., who—at 84—is still in the barn that houses the bottling plant every day.

"Oh, I'm just helping out," he said. "If everyone's away and they need someone to guard the fort, I'm here. I guess I'm like one of those returnable bottles. I just keep showing up again and again."

Problem is, those returnable bottles show up less and less these days.

"I can take you to any antique store around and find one of the bottles for sale for $3 easy," said Tom Conner, delegate for the family's fourth generation. "People have found them as far south as Georgia, but they don't do us any good down there.

"Unfortunately, people just don't return anymore. For most customers, a 10-cent deposit on a bottle isn't worth the trouble of bringing it back to the store, and for us, it costs 42 cents to replace that 10-cent returnable, so unless we use a bottle at least four times, we lose money on it."

And cost aside, it isn't like the returnable bottles are easy to come by.

"We have a bottle broker who travels all over the world," Tom, said, "and the only place he could find that still makes the kind of bottles we use is on the island of Trinidad, and even with them, they only make them every three or four years, so when they're in a manufacturing mood, we have to be in a buying mood."

Even with the changes, Squamscot's customers are still in a buying mood. Brand loyalty may be dying, but it ain't dead yet, not in the restaurants and stores that stock any of Squamscot's 18 flavors.

You can find them at Dante's Spaghetti House in Barrington or at the Ship to Shore in Newfields. They're also on the shelves and in the coolers at the Newfields Country Store and at Gerry's Variety in Exeter, simply because customers demand it

"It's a soda we've carried for as long as I can remember," said Alex Booth, from the High Street Grocery in nearby Exeter. "Even as a kid when I came in here, it was always on the shelf.

"People swear by it," he added, "especially their golden ginger ale. They say it tastes 'more real' than a lot of other brands. It's garnered such a following, I couldn't even think of not carrying it in the store."

And there's more in store for the customers now, what with the switch from a seven-ounce to a 12-ounce bottle. For many businesses, that kind of packaging shift would create havoc with the production line, but not at Conner Bottling.

Any of the three Conners on hand—Alfred, Tom or Dan—can handle the classic 1938 Dixie bottling unit like it's an old friend. In many ways, it is, and for all of the clatter, there's a comfort to the rhythmic "ka-ching, ka-ching" as it fills and caps the long, colorful line of lemon-lime filled bottles.

You still need an old-fashioned bottle opener to get at the soda inside, but the Conners are experimenting with a twist-off cap. They're also experimenting with new flavors—as if 18 isn't enough—but that's a constant with the Conners.

"We like to try them out on family and friends, even store owners," Dan said. "It's like, 'Here. Try this. See what you think.' We did an orange cream soda a while ago, and it tasted just like a Creamsicle. They even have a maple flavor now, so we could make a maple soda if we wanted to. Me, I'll take black cherry."

He'll also take Conner Bottling in some new directions, if he has his way.

"He's got some good ideas," said Tom. "Right now, we don't go too far with our distribution, but Dan has plans. He'd like to see it all over the state, and I'm glad he does. I think we're the only independent soda bottler left in New Hampshire, and that's why I want it to say 'Made in New Hampshire' right on the cases.

"We worked hard to find clear bottles because the colors are so great we want them to show through, and if micro-brewed beer is all the fashion, then why not a locally produced soda? It's not a Coke or a Pepsi, but it's a premium product. It's homemade. Pure sugar. No corn sweeteners, and it has the best flavors we can buy."

An irreverent soda lover might even say it's the *real* thing.

(10/16/98)

The ecclesiastical cottage known as Camp Saint Omer may be vanishing, but the memories of the chapel will live on forever around Lake Umbagog. (Photo Courtesy of Ovide A. Lamontagne)

Camp Saint Omer

AS ALWAYS THIS TIME OF YEAR, except for the chill wind blowing off the water, there's a seasonal calm on the shores of Lake Umbagog. Why, if you cocked an ear to the air, you wouldn't even know there's a demolition project underway.

It's a quiet undertaking.

It always is when nature reclaims a campsite.

And, in spite of its ecclesiastical stature, even a place called "Camp Saint Omer" has no special dispensation when it comes to the laws of nature.

For newcomers to this North Country lake, the weathered bungalow is now nothing more than an attractive nuisance—a run-down shack in a pristine wildlife preserve—but for folks who remember the camp, its founder and its purpose, the demise of the cottage signals the end of a bygone era.

That era began in the 1920s when a legendary parish priest carved out a simple spot in the wilderness. However, what Father Omer Bousquet intended as a modest retreat for priests would, in time, become one of the most unique houses of worship in all of America.

Then again, Father Bousquet was a unique priest.

"I won't say he was the mayor of Berlin, but he picked the person who was going to be," said former Bishop Odore Gendron.

Bishop Gendron should know. His first posting was as an apprentice to Father Bousquet at Berlin's Guardian Angel Parish back in 1947. For a priest in search of a mentor, it was an eye-opening experience.

"He'd see a guy working on his roof on a Sunday and he'd make him come down. He'd tell him, 'You don't work on Sunday.' Then on Monday morning, Father Bousquet would show up with a crew to help the man finish the job.

"And the Brown Company? He wouldn't let them take their trucks through the parish on a Sunday. It was his rule. He really had a lot of power, and he used it for his people," Bishop Gendron said.

In addition to power, the man had energy and insight.

To help parishioners finance their homes, he started a credit union where he insisted that business be conducted in French, *s'il vous plait.* He also helped found the area's first private high school—the Notre Dame School—and, borrowing against his own life insurance policies, he helped build the first indoor arena for ice hockey in Berlin.

"And back then, they didn't have a machine to clean the ice, so you know how we did it, don't you?" asked Bishop Gendron. "He had the novice priests go out and sweep the ice with brooms."

When World War II dawned, Father Bousquet knew meat would soon be in short supply, so he built chicken coops and started a turkey farm to feed his own flock. Later, when those new-fangled electric refrigerators drove the ice companies out, he formed teams to harvest ice from the lake for those who couldn't afford such luxuries.

"The group spent countless hours in the bitter cold of the winter to harvest the thick ice on the upper Androscoggin," wrote Richard Pinette, a North Country historian and author of *Northwoods Echoes.* "This priestly man of many accomplishments could not be distinguished from the other volunteers as he labored on the ice, an old black fur hat pulled down over his ears."

Labors like that made Father Bousquet savor his free time, and when his floating refuge—a small house boat—sank in winter storage near the Errol Dam, he set about creating a more permanent place for priestly leisure.

First he secured a piece of land on the shores of what is known as Leonard Pond, then he resurrected his house boat. Once it was afloat, he towed it to the site, jacked it into the air and built a cottage beneath it. The once-sunken house boat was now the second floor of a lakeside retreat, accessible only by boat.

That recreational purpose alone would have justified its existence, but always mindful of his flock, Father Bousquet petitioned the Bishop for permission to offer Catholic Masses at what became known as Camp Saint Omer.

To accommodate worshippers, Father Bousquet fashioned a rustic chapel just off the cottage's living room, complete with altar and tabernacle. He then passed word around the lake about Sunday

Mass, but even a man so willful as Father Bousquet had to bow to Mother Nature when it came time to schedule services.

"The Mass? That came a half hour after the fog lifted," said Bishop Gendron. "There was no point in starting it at 10 o'clock if people couldn't get there, so we'd wait for the fog to clear. Sometimes it might be as late as 11:30, but people knew."

As the morning fog rolled off the shallow waters, the lake came alive with a flotilla of boats, hailing from points like Molls Rock and Metallak Island and Tidswell Point.

"Long moveable benches were then placed in the living room facing the wide chapel doors which had been opened," Pinette reported. "Sunday after Sunday, the congregation filled those crude benches."

And they filled those benches with more than their posteriors.

"Father Bousquet would never accept money for an offering," said another protege, Father Leo St. Pierre, "so the parishioners would stuff $10 bills in the benches and hide them around the chapel. Ovide Lamontagne was one of them."

That would be Dr. Ovide A. Lamontagne, who spent many a weekend at "St. Omer's On The Lake."

"Later on, a lot of people would bring fresh hornpout and pickerel as part of their offering too," laughed Lamontagne, whose first visit to the camp back in 1941 is one he will never forget.

"Every day they were there, all of the priests would say Mass, one at a time, and since I was an altar boy, I got stuck serving Mass for five priests," he moaned. "I didn't even have a chance to do any fishing, so the next morning, I got up very early, took a boat and hid on the other side of the island so I could do some fishing."

His experience was typical of visitors to Camp Saint Omer, but even in this remote place, change was inevitable. In 1954, the opening of St. Pius Church in Errol drew away many of the worshippers, and understandably, much of the charm of the place was lost when its founder, Father Bousquet, passed away in 1958. Gradually, the cabin has fallen into disrepair.

"Eventually, what's left may have to be taken down," said Paul Casey, manager of the Lake Umbagog National Wildlife Refuge where the camp sits. "It's deteriorated to the point where it can never be restored, and it's really become a liability."

Fortunately, not every vestige of the camp will be lost.

Just two weeks ago, Pinette returned to the camp and retrieved the pieces of the tabernacle that had been demolished by vandals.

Since then, by his own hand, he has painstakingly restored it to its original condition.

"I glued it and sanded it and next summer, I'm going to put it on display at St. Pius," Pinette said. "It was a special place, and I think it's a precious little relic."

For those who fished and worshipped there, it's as precious as the memories of Father Bousquet and the up-country retreat known as Camp Saint Omer.

(11/6/97)

The Sporting Life

LEAVE IT TO MIKE LUPICA, perhaps America's leading sports commentator, to sum up the problems of his beat in an extremely succinct manner. He does this in a new book that makes these central, light-hearted points about professional sports:

1. Owners are scum.
2. Players are scum.
3. We, the fans, are dumber scum—numbskulls, even—for allowing ourselves to be manipulated by these egomaniacal, money-grubbing mercenaries who only think of supporters as a type of intimate apparel that goes into the laundry pile after the game.

Not that Mike is bitter.

Oh, he is, but it's more than that. He's *Mad As Hell,* which just happens to be the title of his new book.

Now, language like that might have got him in hot water with the brothers at Bishop Guertin High School back in 1970, but back in 1970, you didn't have a disingenuous dolt like Art Modell moving his football team from Cleveland to Baltimore for a king's ransom. You didn't have a semi-psychotic creep like Albert Belle getting $10 million a season from the Chicago White Sox and you weren't paying $32—that's THIRTY-TWO DOLLARS!—for four hot dogs and four beers at a new Boston sports arena that should rightfully be called the Fleece Center.

Now I'm *Mad As Hell.*

"And don't think we're alone," said Lupica, whose darkly funny book—both profane and profound—is subtitled "How Sports Got Away from the Fans And How We Can Get It Back."

"I think sports fans today feel totally disconnected with the games they love," he said. "We should be living in a golden age of sports.

Nashua native Mike Lupica fostered a fan revolt when the nationally known sportswriter launched his hardbound attack on the hide-bound sporting establishment. (Photo Courtesy of G.P. Putnam's Sons)

There is more sports available to the average fan than at any time in history, but it's like we're trapped in an abusive relationship."

That disaffection—anger, really—is what Lupica addresses in his new book, which is soaring onto best-seller lists around the country.

He could have done it in his column in the *New York Daily News* or in "The Sporting Life" column he writes for *Esquire* magazine. He could have done it on ESPN, where he is a regular panelist on "The Sports Reporters," but instead, he chose to make it the topic of his ninth book.

Not bad for a 44-year-old guy who got his start covering high school sports for the *Nashua Telegraph.* His wages? Five bucks per story, but trust me when I say that his salary—like pro hockey and Major League baseball—has expanded many times since then.

His influence has grown just as rapidly, so instead of flexing his muscles on the field—which he did as a slender football-playing, hoop-shooting, cross country-running athlete at Bishop Guertin—he's flexing his muscles off the field.

He's using those muscles and his media clout to rally fans behind a number of proposals that would be staggering if they didn't make so much sense. Here are a few:

- Ticket prices will be tied to a team's win-loss record.
- If a star player gets thrown out of the game, fans get their money back.
- Owners sign "prenuptial agreements" with a city when they buy a team. Try to move it and they lose it.
- Any professional franchise owner who asks a city to build a stadium will be sentenced to death.

Okay, I made up the last one but it does have merit. Tell me you wouldn't like to flip the switch on Marge Schott? George Steinbrenner? Or pinhead Paul Gaston, who still has the gall to refer to his Celtics—no, *our* Celtics—as "championship driven"?

"I don't think there's any question that the average fan knows a lot more about sports than the average owner," Lupica said. "These are guys who have made 27 different kinds of fortunes in their other lives, but as soon as they buy a team, they act like complete morons.

"Someone asked me what the owners will think about this book, and the truth is I absolutely do not care," he added. "This book is *about* them, not for them. I wrote this for the fans."

So ultimately—not that this should prevent you from buying the book and forming your own conclusions—what does he think we fans should do?

"I really think the time is right for a real, live national sports organization for the fans," he said. "We had one once. Ralph Nader started it in 1977. It was called FANS. The 'Fight to Advance Nation's Sports.' The only problem is that Dennis Rodman has had hair colors that lasted longer.

"Still, I think with the right leadership, that type of an organization can be as effective as NOW has been for the women's movement."

Even on that upbeat, hopeful note, there is a hint of resignation in Mike's voice when he talks about the state of sports. For all of its faults, it is still his passion—a passion he shares with his father, Benedict Lupica, who will prowl the fairways at Nashua Country Club until the snow drives him indoors—but he also knows that things will never be as simple or as joyful as once they were.

And now that he has become an advocate for the fans—("I didn't volunteer. It was more like a battlefield commission")—he is being swamped with their beefs and complaints, the overflowing rage of this disaffected age.

"The funny thing is, I always came to this looking to celebrate sports," he said. "It's just that sports keeps making it so damned hard."

(11/21/96)

Rene Gagnon

IT WAS BACK IN OCTOBER. They asked me to speak at a breakfast for the DARE program, so I wrote a speech about how kids need heroes and role models. It seemed appropriate.

I figured I could talk about some people I admire, local folks who overcame some hurdles to make their mark in the world. A lot of the names are probably familiar to you. Some are in this book—like Richard McDonald and Grace Metalious, and to me, they're what hometown heroes are all about.

The speech went over well enough, I guess. People laughed when they were supposed to laugh and they applauded when it was time. Looking back on it, I realized I only made one mistake.

I forgot Rene Gagnon.

We do that a lot around here.

His image is frozen in the memory of every American who was alive in 1945 and, for those of us who've come along since, he's part of an indelible national symbol, yet somehow, we often forget to claim him as one of our own.

That won't happen anymore.

At 2 P.M. today, the Memorial Day parade will step off on Elm Street, and by 3 P.M., it's expected to wind its way to Victory Park. That's where they're going to unveil a monument to Rene Gagnon. After 50 years, he's finally getting some recognition where it matters most—in his hometown.

It's a symbolic gesture, to be sure—Rene died in 1979—but he learned the value of symbols on Feb. 23, 1945. That was the day he joined with four other U.S. Marines and a U.S. Navy corpsman and helped plant a flag in a volcanic ash heap called Mount Suribachi on the island of Iwo Jima.

Like all combat soldiers, these six were striving toward a com-

It took 50 years, but Manchester finally has a monument to commemorate Rene Gagnon's role in the historic flag raising at Iwo Jima. (Photo Courtesy of Mrs. Rene Gagnon)

mon goal, but not with weapons of war. They were armed instead with the most powerful symbol of all—a flag—and the unforgettable image captured by AP photographer Joe Rosenthal made them symbols unto themselves.

The only problem? No one knew who they were.

Rosenthal had taken a series of photos that day and dispatched his film without ever seeing the finished product. When the photo began running on front pages all over America—it showed up in *The Manchester Leader* on Feb. 26—everyone wanted to know their names.

War has little patience, however, for the vagaries of public relations, and, as if to punctuate the savagery of the fighting on Iwo Jima, three of the six were dead within a week of the flag raising. Mindful of morale on the homefront, military officials tracked down the survivors—a Pima Indian from Arizona named Ira Hayes, U.S. Navy Pharmacist's Mate John Bradley from Appleton, Wisconsin, and Rene Gagnon—and immediately ordered them stateside.

Even in a more innocent media age, Rene made great copy. He was right out of Queen City central casting—a French-Canadian kid who had to leave Central High School after two years to work in the mills. He tried to join the U.S. Navy at 17 but was refused for high blood pressure. When he finally got into the U.S. Marine Corps, he kept a picture of his sweetheart—Pauline Harnois—in his helmet, and on the way home, he told reporters he couldn't wait to taste his mom's cooking again.

The reason for his homecoming wasn't entirely sentimental. Along with Hayes and Bradley, he was sent on a barnstorming tour of America. Thanks in part to the star power of the Iwo Jima veterans, the Seventh War Bond Drive raised $220 million for the war effort.

By August of 1945, the media crush began to subside. Shortly after V-J Day, Rene was back in the Pacific in combat fatigues, serving with U.S. occupational forces in China. After his discharge in 1946, he was back home with Pauline—America had dubbed her "the sweetheart of Iwo Jima"—and he was back in the spinning room at Chicopee Manufacturing. He couldn't have been farther away from the spotlight.

And he couldn't have been happier.

"To tell you the truth, he was uncomfortable about all that hero stuff," said Omer Gagnon, a childhood friend from St. George's School and The Corporation who saw plenty of action himself at Omaha Beach and Salerno. "The way we saw it, the only hero was a dead hero. They're the ones who gave their lives for their country."

Attention still came Rene's way—there was even a cameo role in the John Wayne film *Sands of Iwo Jima*—yet there were subtle twists of fate, strange mergers of chance and coincidence that seemingly conspired against him.

In the historic photo itself, Rene is largely obscured by the figure of John Bradley, and it wasn't the last time he would be denied his moment in the sun.

Even in the history books, his legacy is frequently garbled. In *Iwo Jima: Legacy of Valor,* for instance, author Bill D. Ross describes Rene as being from "New Hampshire's Green Mountains."

But most importantly, it was when his moment of glory was at hand in his hometown that the fates intervened most cruelly.

When the U.S. Marine Corps ordered him home in April of 1945, the Queen City was in a frenzy. The reception planned in his honor was described as "the biggest homecoming welcome in the history of Manchester." First there was to be a banquet at the Carpenter Hotel, then an evening parade down Elm Street followed by a massive gathering at Bronstein Park.

Dignitaries throughout New Hampshire were clamoring to share the stage with Rene Gagnon. Legionnaires and Cub Scouts alike were lobbying for spots in the parade and for a solid week, the newspaper whipped the city into a patriotic lather. Just when it seemed like his day would never come, it arrived at last. April 12, 1945.

And Franklin Delano Roosevelt died.

The crowds that had lined Elm Street waiting to cheer Rene Gagnon stood in stunned silence as police cars with bull horns broadcast the tragic news. The celebration was canceled. Before it began, Rene's party was over.

Only now, some 50 years later, is he getting his due.

Maybe he would have preferred it that way. After all, he once told a reporter "I'd rather face another invasion operation than go on the bond tour," but in his absence, people like Hubie McDonough Jr. and Don Duhamel and Mike Lopez have made certain that future generations will know of his special place in American history.

For the record, Rene Gagnon is buried in Arlington National Cemetery. His body lies in Section 51 Grave 543—just one more headstone in a sea of 181,000 identical white markers—but as of May 29, 1995, he will be remembered in Manchester forever thanks to the monument that stands, fittingly enough, in the shadow of the American flag.

(5/29/95)

There's Nun Better

WHEN JON THOMAS SAID he was waiting for Lorraine Doucet to give her blessings to his latest batch of beer, he wasn't kidding.

Lorraine is a nun.

But he wasn't after any kind of ecclesiastical endorsement. No, sir, he was after a totally secular seal of approval from a woman who just happens to be one of the leading microbiologists in New Hampshire.

Just don't call her the "Beer Nun."

Brewers like Jon Thomas do, and they do so in tones that border on the, well, on the reverential, but it's just that . . .

"I just don't know what the older sisters in the order would think of that," said Sister Lorraine, who belongs to the Sisters of the Holy Cross and also serves on the faculty at UNH-Manchester.

Since March, she also has served in an advisory capacity with New Hampshire Custom Brewers, a Manchester-based microbrewer that is now bottling and distributing an adult beverage called Loon Pale Ale.

It's her task to make sure that the beer (and the brewery itself) meets and exceeds the highest sanitation standards, for which I—speaking on behalf of devout beer drinkers—can only say, God bless her.

And now that the subject of God has come up, you should know that there are serious longstanding ties between religion and malt beverages. There's even a Trappist monastery in the Netherlands that's totally devoted to the brewing of beer, a circumstance, that, if not for that vow of chastity thing, might have made me rethink my entire career path.

Those monks believe their gift to God is making great beer. It

If you want an expert to make sure your beer will go to the head of the class, there's none better than Sister Lorraine Doucet. (Union Leader Photo by Bob LaPree)

took a great friend to convince Sister Lorraine to use her same gift toward that same end.

"Certainly my being a nun made me tentative about going into this field," she admitted. 'What would people think?' I asked myself. But a friend said, 'You have a skill that people need. You have to use it,' and so . . ."

And so she did, joining that friend, F. Woody Thornton, at Anheuser-Busch in Merrimack, where she spent eight years furthering her research into bacteria that spoils beer.

"The microorganisms are not pathogenic to humans," she explained, "but they can spoil the beer, so ultimately, the impact is financial. It can be disastrous for a microbrewer to lose a whole batch of beer. They run on such a small profit margin that one bad batch can break them."

To prevent that from happening, Sister Lorraine tests the grain. She tests the mash. She tests the pre-beer called "wort." Then she tests the brewing vessels and the pipes and the valves and the bottling equipment and she even tests the bottles. What she's looking for are twin culprits, *pediococci* and *lactobacili*.

"It may seem strange," she said, "but those same bacteria are found in yogurt. It's just that they're good for yogurt and bad for beer."

And bacteria that's bad for beer is bad for business, which is why she also has helped quality microbrewers like Nutfield in Derry, the Stark Mill in Manchester and Lucknow, which is located at Castle Springs in Moultonborough.

"What she's doing is giving us little guys advantages that only the big brewers have had before now," said Mike McDonald, head brewer at Nutfield. "A lot of brewers don't have extremely strong scientific backgrounds, so she lets us use her expertise and her lab and her equipment at the university so we can get the sanitation essentials down."

While Sister Lorraine's work with the brewers may seem a bit unconventional, it vividly illustrates the university's efforts to increase involvement with the business community, according to Dean Karol LaCroix.

"It's very consistent with the mission of a public institution, which is not only teaching and research but also service," she said. "Something like this can lead to field trips, internships and other collaborative projects with industry, which are things we encourage with our students and our faculty."

Eventually—in keeping with that whole academic "publish or perish" thing—Sister Lorraine, a Ph.D., hopes to publish the results of her research. No doubt, there will be a battallion of brewers waiting on her every word, brewers like Art Lyford.

"If you're going to ask people to pay a premium price, you have to make sure you give them a premium product," said Lyford, the CEO of New Hampshire Custom Brewers. "Sister Lorraine makes sure we do that.

"I've met a lot of microbiologists in my other job," added Lyford, who doubles as a dentist in Hollis, "but very few who have the contagious enthusiasm she brings to a project like this."

In addition to her enthusiasm, she also brings a dignity to the proceedings. She isn't like a teacher presiding at a frat party. She's a professional who's bringing professionalism to the microbrewers.

"For one thing, I'm a Manchester girl," she said, "and I'm interested in keeping Manchester vital, whatever the industry. In this case, when I heard the brewery was opening, I walked over, knocked on the door, introduced myself and offered my services."

Religious services? Not in this case, but the beer itself is heavenly.

(6/26/97)

Let the Chips Fall . . .

EVERY ARTIST HAS HIS TOOLS. Michelangelo had his hammer and chisel. Van Gogh had his brush and palette. And Tom Worcester has his chain saw.

It's a real chain saw, too. It's not one of those glorified electric carving knives those "artists" use out west. That's not Tom's style. Why, if he had a mind to, on those rare occasions when he takes a break from sculpting with his chain saw, Tom could use it to put up a cord of wood. Sometimes, he does just that.

The proof is all around his home in Hopkinton, a log cabin—naturally—that is nearly engulfed by the rugged-but-still-delicate sculptures he creates every day.

There is no official designation to be had—not like poet laureate, for instance—but it says here that Tom may be the finest chain saw sculptor in the world. In our own little corner of that world, you may have seen him work his magic at the Deerfield Fair. Come August, you can catch him at the gathering of the League of New Hampshire Craftsmen at Mount Sunapee.

Just listen for the roar and look for the crowd.

He *always* draws a crowd. And he knows why.

"There's a constant danger in what I do," he said. "But, if there wasn't a danger, I don't think people would watch me. I'm sure some people have always wanted to see me hurt myself in some far-off corner of their brains—like at motorcycle or car races—but I've always managed to cheat my public when it comes to that."

That's the *only* way he cheats them.

The show—which is free—is priceless. It's just Tom and a hunk of wood and a chain saw inside a wire cage. When he comes out, there's a statue left behind. Maybe it's a bear, maybe it's an eagle,

He's carved out a remarkable niche for himself with his chain saw sculptures, but Tom Worcester uses a hand-held electric router to bring out the fine details. (Union Leader Photo by Bob LaPree)

maybe it's Uncle Sam. It's an act he's staged all over the country. For years, at the behest of chain saw manufacturers, Tom went barnstorming from coast to coast. He was famous, but he found that fame—by itself—was unfulfilling.

"And that's when I learned about the second part of that fame and fortune thing," he said. "They don't necessarily come together. The fame I had. The fortune part was always the part that managed to escape me, but part of that is my fault.

"As an artist, it was hard to put a dollar amount on something I thoroughly enjoyed. It's something I'd be doing anyway, but I learned. Now I get paid for it."

And why did he start doing chain saw sculpting in the first place? He saw it as a kind of physical therapy. See, back in his motorcycling days, Tom managed to break more bones than Evel Knievel—no brag, just fact—and he needed something to get him moving again.

"I had a lot of operations and a lot of recuperations, and I tried to use that time," he said. "Imagine using a chain saw while recuperating? For me, it just seemed to fit. It's the kind of job that lets me come out and work two or three hours, go in and have a cup of coffee, come back out and work in the dooryard and then go back to the chain saw. I do that seven days a week.

"See, if I rest, I rust," he smiled. "Especially at my age. (He's 59.) You're handling a saw that's only so heavy to begin with, but if you don't use it, it gets heavier. I never did figure that out, but when you pick up a saw on Monday, it weighs twice as much as it did before you put it down."

Now, there may not be a lot of empirical evidence to support Tom's theory on *that* one, but much of what he does is grounded in true science.

"Now you take this log," he said, gesturing toward an eight-footer that will one day be a larger-than-life Indian guide. "When a log is first cut, it's 80 percent water, but as the water dissipates, the cutting of the saw leaves a fuzz that becomes very hard and splintery. That would catch on someone's finger if they ran their hand over it.

"One of the first jobs I ever had was to make a sculpture for a children's museum that had a lot of blind visitors, so I had to come up with a way to get rid of all that fuzz and burning it seemed just ideal. I use an acetylene torch, and after I brush away the burnt wood, it makes it smooth to the touch. Then I put on some linseed oil. That replaces a lot of the water and keeps it so the wood doesn't crack."

That wood? It's pine. Always pine.

"It's not a matter of what I like," he said. "The chain saw is just too fast for hardwood, and it will break off any fine details in a piece. The wood's just too brittle."

While pine can be forgiving, the same cannot be said for some of the archaic bric-a-brac Tom has found embedded in his raw materials. Over the years, those discoveries have made him something of a tree archaeologist.

"See now, a fork in a tree is a great harbinger for whiskey bottles, knives, swords, guns. You name it, I've found it. The fork was where people would hide things when they were out in their fields," he explained.

"A farmer would stash a gun or a knife there so if he was out working in his field and someone broke into his house, well then he had something to defend himself. And a whiskey flask? Well, that way, he could always jump off the plow and have a little sip without the wife seeing him."

The problem is, he can't see those things hidden within the tree, so when he works with his saw, he has to be constantly alert, especially if he intends to keep all of his fingers and toes. At last count, he still had the full quota.

"All the logs I get are discards from mills," he said, in case you thought he was intent on deforesting America. "Those modern mills all have metal detectors that the logs pass through. Things like bullets and nails will give off a signal, so they just cull them off. They won't even bother with them, so I get 'em."

And once he gets 'em, he gets to work.

"I have to do it," he said. "I have this thing where I have to carve as much as I can before I die. That's why I'm out here seven days a week. I want to carve more than anyone else ever carved."

His carving isn't limited to logs. On his rare forays into the house, Tom sits at a small work table and empties a jar that's filled with small pieces of deer and elk antler. With tiny hand tools, he carves out beautifully intricate animals and decorative whorls—it's like a landlubber's form of scrimshaw—and the silence of this workplace is a stark counterpoint to the out-of-doors din.

He's equally at home in both worlds.

"I was always told I was a dreamer," said Tom, who notes proudly that he was the first boy ever to take a home economics course at Concord High School. "I'd look at the clouds and the trees and I'd see all kinds of shapes in them. Now, to be able to find those same shapes in a piece of wood is a blessing for me.

"I don't have any other real goals in life, but I think this is a gift that someone gave me. All I have to remember is I'm holding something that's like a bunch of little knives chasing each other around, and if people appreciate what I can do with it, then I have to do it."

(5/27/99)

Flying Lessons

YOU COULD ASK Carl S. Park Sr. if he thinks the new Manchester Airport terminal building should be named after Alan B. Shepard, but given the bond between the two aviators, his response is pretty much a foregone conclusion.

Not that he's going to hold his breath.

"It's funny," he said, "but it seems like the folks up there have forgotten about everything that happened at the airport before 1940."

He says "up there" because these days, Carl's in New Port Richey, Florida, on the Gulf Coast just north of Tampa. In many ways, however, the man who taught America's first astronaut how to fly has never really left the skies above Manchester.

For 44 years, he made his living in those skies as a commercial pilot and flight instructor, and when he wasn't in the air himself, he was on the ground making sure others could be.

In 1939, he ran the show at what was then known as Manchester Municipal Airport. He was the co-owner of Granite State Airways, but to him, the business was more than a living. It was his life. You hear talk about how some folks eat, drink and sleep flying, but for Carl, it's more than just talk. He actually slept at the airport.

"When I lived out there, we had runway lights, but they weren't automatic," he said. "For the pilots though, it was a known fact that if they circled the field and jazzed their motors, that was the way to wake me up.

"I'd go out in my underwear and run up the stairs to the tower so I could switch on the lights for them to land. I did that for three years. It sounds funny today, but that's how it was."

It does sound funny, especially when you consider what Manchester Airport has become. This year, 1.8 million passengers will pass through the $65 million terminal on flights bound for major hubs

Back when he was flying his single-engine aircraft over Southern New Hampshire, Carl S. Park Sr. didn't know he would help send America's space program soaring too. (Photo Courtesy of Carl S. Park Sr.)

like Baltimore, Chicago, Orlando, Philadelphia, New York and Washington, D.C.

That's a far cry from the early '30s, when Carl was skipping classes at West High School so he could take flying lessons from Pete Goldsmith. In the end, his fixation on aviation prompted him to quit school.

"I had made up my mind I was going to be a pilot," he said, "so I had to work. I needed all the money I could get for flying lessons."

And how was he going to pay for those lessons?

"When I was in high school, there was this big band called Lou Joubert and his NBC Orchestra, and they put out feelers for a drummer, so I went to the audition," Carl said. "I had this beautiful set of drums that I was buying on time. I think I was paying $28 a month for them. In fact, my mother had to sign the note for me.

"Anyway, after the audition, Lou came up to me and said, 'Well, I guess I'll hire you.' I was thrilled, and then he brought me back to earth. He said, 'You're a lousy drummer, but that set of drums will look great on my stage. Besides, I can teach you how to play the drums.'"

A ringing endorsement? Hardly, but it was a job. Carl took it. By the time he won his pilot's license and then his instructor's license, he even managed to merge his vocations.

"We played three nights a week all over New England," he said, "so I'd give flight lessons six or eight hours a day, then I'd get in my tuxedo and fly to wherever we were playing. That airplane came in real handy ."

So did his instructor's license. In 1940, that's what enabled him to take an eager youngster from Derry under his wing, if you'll pardon the expression.

"I didn't know Alan Shepard from a hole in the ground, but this kid came in with a great big grin and you could just tell he was a good kid," Carl said. "He said he didn't have much money but he wanted to learn to fly and he wanted to know if there was anything he could do to get flying lessons.

"I told him if he'd wipe down the airplanes and keep the place clean, I'd give him flying lessons instead of pay. I worked it out so I'd pay him double what he would have made in cash so he could get more lessons."

Alan Shepard often acknowledged the arrangement.

"When I was 13 or 14, 1 started riding my bicycle to the Manchester Airport on Saturdays," he once told *Yankee* magazine. "I would help push airplanes out of the hangars. Sweep out the hangars. They'd fly me around Manchester and down to Derry in a little single-propeller Stinson Voyager or Reliance. I was hooked."

Of course, Admiral Shepard was just one of Carl's many prominent flight students. His alumni group ranged from Blake's Creamery heiress Bernice (Blake) Perry—the first woman to fly solo in Manchester—to Iwo Jima hero Rene Gagnon. Other pupils who made their mark included his own son, Capt. Carl S. Park Jr.—who went on to command the Naval Air Propulsion Center—and Federal Aviation Administration operations inspector Demetrious Copadis, who also authored an early aviation column in *The Union Leader* called "Slips and Spins."

Carl made headlines of his own in 1962 when he provided golf legend Jack Nicklaus—who was running late for a local match with Celtics star Bob Cousy, actor Bob Sterling and State Am champ Joe Gryzwacz—with a bird's eye view of the Manchester Country Club.

Nicklaus fired a 72 that day, and in assessing his performance, *Union Leader* sports columnist Leo E. Cloutier gleefully dubbed Carl "The Flying Caddy."

Of course, Carl's life in aviation wasn't all gentle tail winds. For one thing, on New Year's Day in 1941, the federal government—anticipating war—seized his entire operation at Manchester Airport in the name of national security.

His compensation? Zip.

"After the war, I tried to get it back but by then, it was Grenier Field and they wouldn't let me in," he said, "so I bought three farms over on Route 3A in Hooksett"—one was the Butternut Farm—"and built my own airport. I even plowed and leveled the land myself. It wasn't too good to me, but it was mine."

He kept that venture aloft until 1973. A year later, he and his wife, fellow West Sider Millie (Siddall) Park, flew south toward retirement.

Sadly, after 19,000 hours in the air, Carl's flying days are over.

He's 85 now and his eyes aren't what they used to be, but nearly 60 years ago, they saw somcthing special in a young man named Alan Shepard, and because of his vision, we all view the world a little differently.

(9/14/98)

About the Author

JOHN CLAYTON, a native of Manchester, New Hampshire, is a reporter and columnist for *The Union Leader.* In addition to numerous awards for sportswriting and investigative reporting, he was named "Writer of the Year" by the New Hampshire Press Association in 1997 and in 1998, he was honored as "Columnist of the Year" by the New England Associated Press News Editors. Clayton is also the Emmy award-winning host of "New Hampshire Crossroads" on New Hampshire Public Television. This is his fourth book.